White Man's Tears Conquer My Pains

My World War II Service Story

HENRY BADGETT

Copyright © 2014 Henry Badgett
All rights reserved
First Edition

PAGE PUBLISHING, INC.
New York, NY

First originally published by Page Publishing, Inc. 2014

ISBN 978-1-62838-941-8 (pbk)
ISBN 978-1-62838-942-5 (digital)

Printed in the United States of America

CONTENTS

Preface 5

Chapter One: The Choice 7

Chapter Two: Training Camp 10

Chapter Three: All Aboard 17

Chapter Four: Day of Indoctrination 21

Chapter Five: The Day I Became a Cook 24

Chapter Six: Docking on Midway Island 27

Chapter Seven: Docking on Johnston Island 33

Chapter Eight: Docking at Wake Island 38

Chapter Nine: Service in Guam 44

Chapter Ten: First Assignment in the Philippines 51

Chapter Eleven: Baguio 61

Chapter Twelve: Second Assignment 72

Chapter Thirteen: Field Hospital Stay 76

Chapter Fourteen: Day of Surgery 82

Chapter Fifteen: Beginning of Recovery 86

Chapter Sixteen: Rehabilitation Period 90

Chapter Seventeen: So Long To a Friend 96

Chapter Eighteen: My Final Days at the Hospital 100

Chapter Nineteen: Concluding Thoughts 112

PREFACE

White Man's Tears Conquer My Pains is the story of a young black soldier, fighting for his life in an all-white United States field hospital, in Manila, Philippines. He is filled with the same prejudice he experienced all of his life while trying to support a young wife and child. He wants to prove to the world and to himself that he has something valuable to contribute to society even though he is being honorably discharged as a disabled veteran. This war made him a man.

The title for this story is truly because of a Southern white doctor who saved his hand, his life and helped him learn how to live with prejudice and trust. Doctor May chanced his rank as an officer and refused to cut off his hand in surgery. After trying for three days to help him talk, he finally was able to say "yes sir" and the doctor cried. This still makes him feel good today even though it took place more than sixty-eight years ago.

CHAPTER ONE

The Choice

Every time I look at my right hand, or what's left of it, even at the ripe old age of eighty six, I am reminded of the choice a doctor had to make as I lay near death in a field hospital in Manila, Philippines. I was the only survivor among the group of fourteen soldiers that I led one day into battle with the Japanese in the jungle a few days earlier.

I had known the hatred of racial prejudice my entire life as a male who grew up in the South. I called it bullshit then and I call it bullshit today. I learned to accept it and live with it, but I never liked it. I ridiculed the entire system any time that I could.

I can remember very vividly riding a streetcar in Dallas with a good white friend of mine. Of course, I had to sit in the back while he got a seat in the front section. That didn't stop me from having a conversation with him during the entire ride, as I hollered from the back and he answered me from the front. I always used to tease him, reminding him that even though he got a nice seat in the front of the streetcar, if it were ever in an accident, he would get the worst of it, along with the other white riders. I'm not sure anyone thought of that when they decided to herd the blacks to the back.

I never let the cruelty of racism infect my soul. I've always strived to lead a positive life, and that has served me very well. I have had a great life, and no man or woman of any color can stop me from enjoying what I have or nullify what I have accomplished, despite the forces that wanted to judge me and hold me back based on the color of my skin. I have always treated others with respect and sought that same respect in the way that I carried myself. That has served me well over my near-century of living.

In the army, I had risen to sergeant very quickly because I was appreciated for my brains, my hustle, my integrity, my character, and my warrior spirit.

None of that matters though, on the day I lay there in that hot, humid field hospital while a doctor, a nurse, and several officers discussed my treatment. To some, all that mattered was that I was black, even though it appeared that I was about to give my very life for my country.

I had a feeling that I might not come out of that hospital in the way that I wanted, based on what I had heard around me.

"Why is he in the hospital?"

"He is here because he is an American soldier, and if you don't see him in the same manner, get the hell out of here now!"

"I'm sorry, sir. I truly didn't mean it like it sounded. I made a bad mistake."

I wasn't sure who said what, but I don't think the question was a mistake. It was a different time then. Even though black men served well in the Armed Forces throughout World War II, it was still very difficult for many white men to get their head around the notion of treating us equally in the army, and I can understand their struggles with that concept. What logical sense did it make to treat me, a black man, as an equal, as a true human being, in that field hospital, when back home I was never treated as an equal? Did the geography change the ethics? Sometimes it did, and sometimes it didn't. Old attitudes did not fade away just because we were nearly ten thousand miles from home. I was still a "nigger," and I had been called that a thousand times or more already during my seventeen months of service.

Back to the discussion of my treatment: three or four officers surrounded my bed, along with my doctor and a nurse, who were looking at my schedule and talking about my case as the officers listened. I did not really understand what they were saying, due to my fuzzy state at the time and the terms that they used, which were beyond my knowledge.

One at a time, the officers began to leave the room, leaving a colonel alone with my doctor and a nurse. After he took a couple of steps, the colonel turned to my doctor and said brusquely, "Cut the right hand to the wrist."

My doctor calmly replied, "Sir, I think I can save at least three fingers."

The colonel turned and glared at my doctor, saying, "Save three fingers on a nigger's hand?"

And that's when the doctor had a choice to make.

CHAPTER TWO

Training Camp

It was in San Antonio, Texas, that my odyssey began, taking me from my hometown of Dallas halfway around the world to the jungle in the Philippines. I still look back at my time in the army as the transformative time of my life, the time I became a man. In that way, Daddy was wrong. I didn't become a man simply by impregnating a girl. I became a man as I fought for my country and faced down death—and won.

I stayed in San Antonio for four days after my enlistment on March 7, 1946. Soldiers were restricted from leaving the army base because they were preparing for duty and were not allowed to socialize with civilians during this transition stage. During that time, we soldiers received medical examinations of all sorts, clothing, equipment, supplies, and identification documents.

We were then shipped to Fort McClellan in Anniston, Alabama, one of the busiest forts in the country, where more than a half-million troops were trained for the war. I would spend sixteen weeks of hell there. I was called nigger far more often than my name, my initials, or any other title. As a black man, that word never failed to hurt my ears and cut me to the bone. I boiled inside every time I heard it; I never, ever got used to it. My trainers were all white men, ranking from private to colonel, and they did not care about making black soldiers angry. In fact, they wanted to make us furious, I am sure, so that we would attack our training with twenty times the energy of a normal man.

Every single day, our trainers would pick a different soldier to punish at least twice a week, spreading that punishment to the entire group by making everyone get up late at night or very early in the morning to do a random assignment or difficult exercise. And so began the harshest treatment I had ever experienced in my life. We worked six days a week and had punishments added in constantly, sometimes for wrongs done, sometimes simply because we were in the service.

Despite these hardships, our trainers taught me lessons that would serve me well in future combat, tips about engaging the enemy, and saving your own life while in heavy jungle. I can still remember in detail many of the instructions that these trainers gave. I believe there is a moral for everyone in my experience; even if you are not particularly fond of your instructor in any area of life or business, don't close your ears to what they have to say. You could miss out on a piece of advice that could one day save your life.

For some reason, the trainers always seemed to set me aside and give me special instructions on how to make and follow trails, and how to keep off dry leaves and bushes. Perhaps they knew somehow that I would be leading a group of men through thick jungle within months, half a world away from my home.

Here are a few of the choice nuggets that these trainers passed on to me:

- Always look up into the trees—the enemy might be there.

- Watch for moving bushes.
- When a group of birds is frightened, it often flies east, and it is likely that they were disturbed from a northern or western direction.
- When you shoot your gun into bushes, stay low and hide from open view, hopefully hiding behind something that protects you.
- Always leave a marked trail.
- See anything suspicious? Check it over and over again.
- Never build a fire near dry bushes or grass, or in an open area.
- Never leave a fire with even one ember still hot or smoking.
- Before advancing your group, do a detailed survey of the area where you hope to advance. The same goes for where you plan to spend the night in the wild.
- *Always* check in trees for anything unusual.
- Never drink water until you are full.
- Watch your mate or group at all times.

As part of this encyclopedia of knowledge, the trainers also worked on our hearing. They drilled us over and over again on what were real sounds emanating from real sources, and phony sounds emanating from created sources.

I would draw on all of this knowledge within a few months, and I am grateful to this day for the comprehensive training I received on living in wartime conditions in the jungle. If not for this training, I would have quickly been killed, I am sure.

After our first twelve weeks of training, we were issued weekend passes. Most of us went to a little town called Anaheim. I will never forget that first trip there. It seemed that everyone in that town who had something to sell knew exactly how much money each serviceman had to spend, and each person that you came into contact with made sure that they got as much as they could when you dealt with them.

I was standing in the front office at Fort McClellan trying to figure out how I would get to this escape destination when I met two other soldiers. We caught each other's eye and introduced ourselves. I went first, then one said, "I'm Pvt. Wesley Thomas, Dallas, Texas. I had two years of school at Wiley College, got broke, and decided to go into the service and serve enough time and have Uncle Sam help me to finish school." The other soldier announced, "I'm Pvt. Clarence Harris from Fort Worth, Texas. I quit my woman, well, now I can tell the truth: she quit my ass for my best friend, so I decided to join the army and let them take me away from Fort Worth." He laughed.

As we were getting acquainted with one another, another soldier walked up and introduced himself, "I'm Pvt. Richard Harold. Are you guys going on leave?"

"Yes, we are."

"Are you going to Anaheim?"

"Yes."

"I'm going to Anaheim. It will cost you $2 each to ride with me."

"Okay."

We took the ride and had a great time telling jokes and lies, and talking about our families. I could have hung out with this group for the rest of the evening, but the catch was that no women were in the bunch. We were dropped off right in the middle of town, where black people did business and entertained at pool halls and clubs. The restaurants that could serve us were in this part of town too, along with barbershops and churches. It was the center of the black community.

We were able to be served liquor at age eighteen in that little town, so we stepped inside a club and found prices inflated to more than double the usual rate; twenty-five-cent beers went for sixty-five cents to soldiers, due to the jukebox that provided entertainment, which we had to fund.

For another twenty-five cents, you could dance with a lady. One-dollar sandwiches came with a bottle of soda, as did a dollar order of barbecue or chitterlings. Chili went for fifty cents with a bottle of pop; crackers cost you another dime.

Inflated prices aside, I decided to seek out a woman for some serious socializing. I saw a nice-looking one and asked her over to my table. She came over and announced that I would have to dance with her if I wanted to get to know her. I then asked, "Can't I pay you for visiting with me?" She said, "Let me ask the person in charge of us."

She went over to a lady and was told that it would be all right if I wanted to pay her for her time. We agreed on twenty-five cents for each dance she missed or a dollar per hour. I gave her two dollars, and she went back to the lady, who said that was just fine. We sat and proceeded to have a wonderful time together.

Her name was Claurice Evans. I bought her a Royal cola, and I'm sure she felt special getting paid to sit and entertain a young soldier. She didn't think I could dance, but in fact I was a very, very good dancer. After we got to know each other, I asked her to dance. Was she surprised!

I could tell that she was excited to have met a soldier who respected her, bought her drinks, complimented her on her looks, and could dance. We enjoyed a wonderful hour or two together.

Eventually, I looked around and saw one of the guys who had come with me into town. He was sitting alone. I excused myself from Claurice and went over to him. I asked if he was ready to return to camp. He replied, "We are ready when you are." We decided on twenty minutes more, then we would leave.

I returned to my table with Claurice and she asked, "What is going on?" I replied, "We decided to leave in twenty minutes, so I rushed back to have another dance with the most beautiful lady in Anaheim." After that last dance, we sat and laughed and had fun. I knew that I was overpaying her, but I decided to give her another three dollars as a tip. She was ecstatic. She told me that was the most she had ever received from a guy, and that she had enjoyed the best day she could remember at the club. She thanked me and offered a way to get in touch with her when I returned to Anaheim. I told her that I wouldn't be coming back. She asked if I wanted her to take the rest of the day off. I said, "No. Stay and make other soldiers as happy as you made me." She answered, "There are no more soldiers like you." I smiled and said, "Thanks again, Claurice."

The trip back to Fort McClellan by cab was six miles and cost five dollar each for two or more soldiers, eight dollars for one. After midnight, each trip to the base cost ten dollars per trip. After that one visit to Anaheim, I decided to remain on base on weekends, primarily because I saw that town to be so corrupt, prejudiced, and filled with greed that I feared for my life. For instance, if you were a black man, you had to be extremely careful that you were not on the same side of the sidewalk as a white woman. You also could not look directly at a white woman, especially if she had shorts on!

Other indignities based on race included the need to take exact change into any store that you entered. If not, the clerk might just have kept the change and said something like, "Thanks. Now, get the hell out if you don't want anything else."

As for buying anything from a stand, such as a hot dog, hamburger, or even flowers, you would probably have to stand in front of a white man, which could lead to problems. And if you happened to be in line with a white woman, one who was either in front of you or behind you, God only knows what could happen.

All of these tensions grew astronomically after sundown. No black man in his right mind would stay in Anaheim after dark. You can understand why I did not want to bother with all of these potential pitfalls, no matter how much fun I had with Claurice.

This type of negative interaction in American society, despite the fact that I was an American serving my country, led me to request overseas service. I did not want to take the chance of being assigned to a U.S. post, where I would be treated like a prisoner or an animal—or worse. I concluded, rightly I believe, that even if I was in a black unit, I would not be treated well because the black leaders had to play along with this prejudiced system to achieve the ranks that they sought. I could either live in a constant state of anxiety and latent anger, or I could see the world and accumulate traveling experience, learn other cultures, visit exotic places and, most of all socialize with people from different civilizations who treated blacks as human beings. My choice was easy; when I was asked where I would like to be assigned in the army, I applied for overseas duty immediately.

CHAPTER THREE

All Aboard

After nearly eighteen weeks of training in Alabama, I was shipped to the port of embarkation for a departure overseas. That port was Seattle, Washington, where I spent four days receiving medical treatment for overseas travel, documents, clothing, and supplies. It was about 0940 hours one day when we began to board a huge ship. I started to realize that I was getting ready to experience something completely new in my life, an adventure of which I had no prior knowledge, where I would venture into places and situations that I had never known. These thoughts come to you as you walk up that plank and are separated from dry land all of a sudden. The gap between that ship and land might as well have been a hundred miles wide. The distance between your former life and your future is even wider than that when you take the step I did, from boyhood to training to actual fighting.

    I am still thankful for the adventure I had in the service, which began in earnest that day. I was in a way, saying good-bye to being a fairly innocent teenager, a boy from a large family who knew little of the outside world. I was beginning a new life, and I would never look back on my past in the same way again. I don't think it's an exaggeration to say that when you cross that plank, you are stepping from boyhood to manhood. At least, that was the case for me.

To add to the newness of this experience, I did not know a single soul on that ship. I had been the only soldier who had shipped out when I left training camp to catch a train for Seattle. I had no idea what the army was doing with me.

The first item we received upon boarding was a list of instructions about how to get to our living quarters. Those instructions told us that we would receive further directives over the ship's loudspeaker at a special time. In the meantime, we were ordered to unpack and told where to place our clothes and supplies. We were given a bunk number and directed on how to make up our bunk, as well as given commands on unit discipline. We also received a personal identification number. Mine was 5906, a number burned into my memory, and hopefully the memories of a few others in the service, for good reasons.

At 1130 hours, a message from the loudspeaker announced when and where each soldier would go for lunch, according to the ID numbers we had. I proceeded to eat lunch at the appointed time and enjoyed a delicious meal. I immediately met a soldier who was a cook's assistant at the mess hall. He asked me if I would be interested in being a cook on the ship, which surprised me a little because I had never seen a black soldier in the kitchen. I told him I wanted a little time to think about it. He gave me his name and told me how to get in touch with him later. The thought of being a cook had never really entered my mind, and I wanted time to process this request. Another example of me being given a different sort of treatment again caused me to reflect. This actually could serve as a theme for my entire military career: getting into places and positions that few, if any, new black recruits did.

I was assigned to a unit primarily comprised of white soldiers in Detachment One, on the first level of the ship. I thought this was a mistake that would be corrected later, but no one said a word during that first weekend. My unit bunkmates were two black first lieutenants who served as engineers. We introduced ourselves and chatted. I told one of them that I wasn't sure why I was assigned to their cabin. He introduced himself as First Lieutenant Theodore Williams but told me to call him Ted.

"I spend much of my time on an assigned station because my work won't let me choose when I go on duty," he said. After he changed his clothes, he sat back on his bunk as he put on his shoes, and he welcomed me aboard warmly. I thanked him. Then began a conversation that would have a large impact on my later service. It's funny how these chance conversations can play a major role in your future, sometimes even during the first words you exchange with a new acquaintance.

Ted asked, "What do you do when you are just passing time?"

"Sometimes I read a book or just relax."

"Let me show you something." He got up, and then returned with a radio. "Did you ever learn how to use an army radio?"

"No."

He then began to explain the different ways of operating the radio, using code signals to send and receive messages. He also showed me how and when to turn the radio off and on, how to carry it, and how and when it should be kept hidden. We played around with a set of radios for about a half hour, mimicking real radio communication. It was fun and educational, and it's always great when those two things go together. Little did I know that I would be using one of these radios in a life-or-death situation a few months later. That initial session with Ted was my introduction to this form of communication, which I would need to master soon. It was a seemingly random few minutes of fun, but a first step down the track I would rise on in the military. I have found nothing ever really happens by chance.

We eventually talked about Ted's love life, his fondness for engineering and electronics, life at sea, and why he decided to make the service his career. Ted said he planned to serve twenty years, then retire. I said, "I just don't think I would want to give that much of myself, to give up that much privacy."

"That's a wise way of explaining life," he replied. "Do you shoot pool?"

"No, I never really got into that game."

"I have a buddy. I think I'll go pull him out of the bunk and play a game or two." I saw Ted rarely during my month aboard the ship. He was on duty for long hours, as was my other bunkmate.

The white and black soldiers were separated completely on the ship. The Mexicans were considered white and were assigned to Detachment One too. The blacks were assigned to Detachment Two, which always ate second and sometimes discovered that certain dishes were already consumed by the time they arrived at the mess hall. Members of Detachment One always left enough of these dishes behind to let the black soldiers know what they had missed as they looked longingly at the few scraps of dessert or some other treat that remained, yet another reminder of blacks' status as second-class soldiers. I mention this because it would lead to a big day in the course of my military career, a day when I had to earn some respect by dishing out a few knuckle sandwiches.

CHAPTER FOUR

Day of Indoctrination

One day I was on my way back to the unit when I saw some white and black soldiers in a crowded circle throbbing with noise and blocking the hallway. I had to go through this circle to continue on my way; it was unavoidable. When I arrived at the circle, I realized a fight had broken out. As I entered the scrum, a white guy pulled me into the circle and punched me. I instinctively protected myself, and before I knew it, I was in the middle of a fight that I had known nothing about, with an opponent that I did not know from Adam!

After a few minutes of exchanging blows, I got the upper hand, having decked two white guys. All of a sudden, I was in the middle of the circle fighting a large, redheaded man, who I later found out was a sergeant named James Credell, on his way back to Johnston Island in the Pacific. The crowd loudly cheered as we faced off, the only two left standing. We exchanged heavy blows in a tussle that resembled a boxing title match. Suddenly, a group of men grabbed me and took me and Sgt. Credell to a room with three cells. I then realized I was being detained by these security guards, whom I had not been aware of until that time.

Thirty minutes into my incarceration, two officers and three sailors came into the room and introduced themselves as the guard patrols of the ship. I recognized the three sailors as the men who had apprehended me and Sgt. Credell. One of the officers was black, and he asked my name, rank, unit ID, and detachment number. He then inquired, "Henry, in your own words, would you tell us what happened and how you got involved in this conflict?"

"I was coming from the mess hall after lunch and came upon a crowd of mixed soldiers in the hallway I had to pass through. As I tried to pass through the crowd, I was pulled inside the circle, and before I could pass through, I was involved in what looked like a group fight, and ended up fighting this fellow."

"Anything else you would like to add to this?" the officer asked.

"Yes. I am happy it was a clean group fight."

The white officer said, "I most certainly agree with that" and then asked Sgt. Credell what had happened. He said, "A white soldier showed a black soldier the last of a dish of bread pudding that was served at lunch and made some remarks about it; the trash talk went on until a fight was started. I was a part of the trash talk and fight, and all of a sudden Henry was facing me in the circle and we had an 'excuse me, sir' hell of a fight. It was fun, and he is a good person, I know, and I am glad to meet a fellow like that." He then came over to me and shook my hand, saying, "No harm done. It was like it was planned."

The white officer then announced, "Henry, we will review this action and get back to you with the results later. We want you to know there are always better ways to settle things than fighting."

And thus began one of my first friendships on the ship, with one Sgt. James Credell, a man whose respect I earned when I used my fists to make my point. Certainly, there were better ways to settle things than fighting, but sometimes a man has to do what a man has to do. Winning two preliminary bouts and earning a draw with James was vital to getting the respect I needed and deserved on our ship. When you think about it, we men are not much different than those rams that crash into each other on mountainsides around the world. We have to hit each hard a few times to establish who we are and how we will relate to other men. It's kind of primitive, but I think it's still true. That day, everyone learned an important lesson about Henry Badgett: don't touch him in a menacing way unless you want to get into the fight of your life. Throughout my time in the service, I earned respect from a wide variety of people, especially officers. This was the first step in that process. This was a one-time event, thankfully. Later, the way in which I interacted with people, giving them respect while maintaining my own, led to me gaining promotions and status throughout my brief career. I didn't always have to fight my way to the top, but these total knock outs were the start of my leadership role in the army, I believe. I hadn't planned on introducing myself to a large segment of the ship's population by punching people, but that's the way it had to be. I literally had to fight for respect—and I got it.

As for Sgt. Credell, I later learned that he had been a bully during his time in the service, before he met his match in me. The key to our rapid friendship was not only our stand-off in the ring, but our mutual interest in leading men. James had been on the ship for about two weeks before I was, so he also helped me get to know many of the soldiers on board.

My brief fighting career in the army was not only an indoctrination into how to establish one's self in the ship's pecking order, it was an introduction to a wider circle of eventual friends, acquaintances, and contacts. Knowing how to handle myself in a fist fight did not slow my advancement to being a leader, that's for sure.

CHAPTER FIVE

The Day I Became a Cook

After leaving the guard's office I went to my unit and slipped into my bunk to relax. After a couple of hours, an announcement came over the loudspeaker, giving assignments for personnel groups. I was one of the soldiers to get an assignment, which was again announced by ID numbers. I was ordered to have breakfast at 0530 hours and report to a group meeting at 0700.

I met the group the next day and was issued clothing and materials for painting. I did ship maintenance for ten days in a row, from 0730–1730 hour, working a half-day on Saturday, but all day every other day. After the first weekend, I was so tired that I thought I was going to die, and I'm not trying to be overly dramatic. I was the only black worker in the group of twelve, and somehow I was assigned to do all of the overhead work and trim, which is often elevated. If you have ever painted a surface above your head, you know how it feels after just a half-hour of work. Imagine doing that repeatedly over ten straight days. Now you know how I felt and why I say I thought I was going to perish. The pain shot through my neck and shoulders and throbbed up into my head. Working in the mess hall started to look a lot more appealing.

The first weekend of my painting duty, I went to the mess hall and again saw the soldier who had asked me to think about working there. He introduced me to the chef and I was told to come back the next day.

The next day, the chef asked me about my experience around kitchens, and I told him that my uncle owned a restaurant and that I had done work for him as a cook. I had also helped my mother cook for six younger sisters and brothers. My oral resume impressed him during our conversation.

He took me to a large refrigerator room and showed me forty pounds of ground meat. He challenged me, "We have had this meat for about eight days and did not discover it until two days ago. It was under some packages and other stuff and we have to get rid of it in the next couple of days. What could you do with it besides make hamburgers?"

I replied, "If you wanted to make something people would find tasty and desirable, you could make a dish called goulash. It is made with a sauce and/or tomatoes, onions, salt, pepper, ground meat, and a pinch of sugar, which always adds a good taste to beef, made as a stew-type dish. This really helps if the meat is a little old."

He responded, "You are hired today," and he took note of my ID number and other identification. He then made a call to someone and said to me, "Henry, let's talk about scheduling." We agreed on it and I started to work in the kitchen the next Monday at 0330 sharp. He was thrilled that I was going to prevent him from having to destroy a whole lot of old meat.

I instantly became the lead cook because the regular lead cook was ill and the other cooks were assistant cooks. I gained a lot of favor with those guys because I had cooked for a big family and knew how to work with other people in a kitchen, a skill not everyone has. I had a ball giving orders and having people come to me with questions. The chef thought I was fantastic as well. I was working with other people to make the weekly schedule during my first day on the job, and I promptly drafted several other soldiers to help make the goulash for the 160 soldiers on the ship.

It just so happened that a group of about fifteen officers were visiting the ship on special assignment that night. I will never forget the menu; goulash, candied yams, cabbage, carrots, regular loaf bread, and corn bread muffin, Jell-o and cookies for dessert. Everyone loved it.

I worked Monday to Wednesday and Saturdays, but the head cook returned the next Monday and thus ended my brief reign atop the kitchen staff. Even so, the chef told me he would carry me on the schedule for the next week, so I didn't have to worry about being scheduled for any other work. I gave him a hearty, right on! My cooking experience back in Texas had come in handy, winning me a reprieve from the torture of painting ceilings and trim.

In weeks to come, kitchen staff would see me and say, "Wish you were back in the kitchen," along with other similar comments. The kitchen must have been missing a little "Badgett magic" because I also received greetings of "Hello, Chef!" from cooks that I had supervised.

One of my painting buddies came by my table and pointed out in a wise-ass way that I was a much better cook than painter. I replied, "Don't worry. Someday your talent will be discovered."

CHAPTER SIX

Docking on Midway Island

The next day, the officer of the Guard Patrol came by my unit and said that he had been meeting with a group of people that was responsible for entertainment on the ship. He said he hoped that Sgt. Credell and I could meet with this group, which wanted us to put together a boxing program for weekend entertainment. I asked where the equipment and supplies would come from and was told that all would be taken care of by the group.

Sgt. Credell and I met with the group, and it was decided that we would run the program, which included devising the rules for the bouts. We flipped a coin and I was chosen as the manager. We picked two men, one white and one black, to choose fighters by weight class and character, but we reserved the right to make the final decision. Within three days, we were ready to rumble.

We had the bouts announced three times a day over the ship's loudspeaker, and the card commenced on Friday at 1800 hours. We had bouts that lasted three rounds, two minutes per round, and the spectacle was a smashing success. Everyone had a blast, but the real buzz began when it was announced that Sgt. Credell and I would duke it out the following Friday. There was so much hype to this rematch that we agreed to fight one week after our initial extravaganza, but we never got the chance to put the gloves on.

Our minds were not on fun and frivolity when we had a possible attack alert a short time later and were assigned to private safety zones for fourteen hours. When that happened, we ate K rations, those infamous meals that came in a large cardboard box, with a canned entrée and everything from biscuits to chewing gum included. After the alert ended, we had special orders to prepare for the unloading of several personnel from the ship. Just like that, contact with many of the soldiers I had recently met ceased, including interaction with Sgt. Credell and the other white guards. I now interacted exclusively with about twenty-five black soldiers on the ship.

I later learned that our ship spent lots of time eluding Japanese submarines, zigging and zagging in the Pacific to stay out of harm's way. That is why we had several alerts that restricted our movements and the use of lights and appliances on board. We were in far more danger than I ever realized, just another way that my life was spared during my time in the service.

When we docked at Midway Island (so named because it rests half way between North America and Asia in the North Pacific Ocean), a group of white soldiers got off the ship. This island had been the site of what many consider the critical battle in the Pacific, when from June 4–6, 1942, American troops repelled a Japanese attack and turned the tide of the war in that area. The Japanese Navy had never been defeated until that time, and the key to the victory was cracking the Japanese code and discerning their plans for an ambush. The U.S. forces won despite being outnumbered four-to-one in personnel and equipment. The island had been seen as the second most important base for protection of the U.S. west coast, behind only Pearl Harbor, and we all know what happened there.

Midway was also bombed on December 7, 1941, as well as on February 10, 1942, by a Japanese submarine. Midway was a critical base for U.S. subs, as well as a convenient refueling stop for transpacific flights and navy ships. The battle of Midway in June 1942, later popularized in a hit movie starring a superstar cast of Henry Fonda, Charlton Heston, James Coburn, Robert Mitchum, and others, with a score written by John Williams of *Star Wars* fame, saw the good guys sink four Japanese aircraft carriers and destroy hundreds of Japanese aircraft, a loss that their navy never fully recovered from. The U.S. lost the USS Yorktown in the fierce battle, along with many of its own aircraft, but the victory is seen by most historians as the beginning of the end of the Japanese Navy's control of the Pacific Ocean.

Another interesting feature of this island is its spot near the International Date Line, just 161 miles west. That means that as you travel west, you must add one number to the calendar date. When traveling east, you suddenly had an instant savings time of sorts and went back in time one day. None of that mattered to us when we heard large numbers of planes flying over our ship which definitely scared the hell out of this soldier.

At 1835 hours, I received a message via the loudspeaker to report to the guards' room. Sgt. Credell was there and we talked for hours. It was almost unheard of for a white soldier to bid farewell to a black soldier over several hours of conversation, but that's the kind of friendship that Sgt. Credell and I had. We had been restricted from visiting each other's units because of the race regulations that were enforced as part of our limited movement orders, which segregated the detachments. I would have had to say good-bye to many friendships because of these rules, but thanks to my status in the kitchen and role as fight promoter, I was seen a little differently, a phenomenon that would prove true throughout my military career.

Sgt. Credell, whom I will again call James for short, told me about a trip he had taken to Johnston Island on an earlier mission. This island is located about halfway between the Marshall and Hawaiian islands. James said his first mission there had been a nightmare, due to his sea sickness and other trials. To add to the misery of his stomach woes, a soldier named Chuck Gaines, known as a bully and a true pain in the ass, had inhabited the bunk below him and thought it was fun to kick the bottom of James' bunk nonstop.

Chuck had gotten his comeuppance earlier, but he still had a lot of aggravating behavior in him. We all thought he had learned his lesson once and for all when he picked on "Mexican red pepper," Johnny Rios, a former Golden Gloves boxer. Johnny was scrappy and tough, a man who used to drive a gang-brand motorcycle too, such as a model made for the Blue Angels or Tiger Team, some said. He told a lieutenant that he had had enough of Chuck. The lieutenant suggested that Johnny put a boxing ring on the forward deck to end their dispute once and for all. Johnny did so, and he proceeded to cut Chuck to pieces in the ring. To Chuck's credit, every time he got knocked down, he got back up. The lieutenant eventually stopped the fight and probably saved Chuck's life, but Chuck's attitude only improved slightly after that memorable one-sided bout. I steered clear of him, and was thankful that James had given me the low-down on this low-life.

After telling me about how aggravating Chuck had been during the mission to Johnston Island, which didn't surprise me in the least, James said that he felt a little better because looking out of his portal, he could see Johnston Island, after a full eighteen days at sea. I looked out and could also see the island, which was about forty miles away. It's hard to describe what it's like to only see the outside world through a porthole. You don't see much even if you can see very far on the horizon, and you certainly never know what is taking place above you, below you or beside you. When you hear strange noises in any of those directions, you can be smothered with genuine fear, even if you are not an especially fearful person. It is not an ideal way to see the world, trust me, and it is no way to live for an extended period of time. Thankfully, I lived to tell about it.

I asked James, "If you dislike Johnston Island so much, why are you going back?" He said, "I know how the system operates and I know the players and dealers, plus I am promised second lieutenant after about four months more. This is a field promotion, which makes it quicker." I nodded my understanding and bid him good night, leaving my old sparring partner to return to my unit. James had asked for special permission to say good-bye to me; it was a wonderful, cherished gift that I will never forget. One of the true gifts of military service is the relationships that you form with your fellow soldiers, even if they are brief and you never see each other again.

Often when I returned to my bunk, I wondered how I came to be assigned to share quarters with two officer/engineers who were also Board Members of Operations. I think the only reason I was lucky enough to bunk with these men was because of the limited space for black soldiers. Why was I chosen? That's part of the wonder of this memoir.

The forty black servicemen on the second and third levels had filled those levels to capacity. The white personnel had very little contact with these men of color because the blacks handled the merchandise, equipment, and supplies, loading and unloading them as needed at different locations. The races did intersect a bit at the boxing matches that I helped to organize, but it's a true shame that these men could not have had more interaction, other than in a ring with gloves on. Both races would benefit from spending time with one another to build a true group effort, as we see in many segments of society today.

The army was integrated in 1946, but as I've told many people, we blacks were in the army by law, not because the whites wanted us there. It wasn't until President Truman's Executive Order 9981 on July 26, 1948, that racial discrimination was banned in the Armed Forces, an order that led to the end of the segregation that I am describing.

We planned on docking at Johnston Island the next day, if no surprises came upon us. We had dinner at 1830 hours, as usual, I recall, and I showered, wrote a couple of letters, and called it a night soon afterward. I slept well and woke at 0530 hours, looked out my porthole and saw nothing but water. At 0610 hours, the loud speaker wished us all a good morning and told us that everything was beautiful.

CHAPTER SEVEN

Docking on Johnston Island

I had breakfast at 0630 and the ship docked at 0950. At 1015 hours, the loudspeaker announced that certain personnel would report to the East side, opening slide-07, dressed in maintenance uniforms with hand gloves, to begin work at 1040. The eighteen names called included mine. I tell this story because it illustrates the grace that was shown to me as a black man, and proves again that the races can work together when needed. I also tell it as a reminder to myself that many other black men were capable of leadership in many forms in the army in 1946, but for some reason I was the only one chosen on that ship for such responsibility, and that responsibility would only grow in days to come. Perhaps it was a bit like the Parable of the Talents in the Bible. I did not bury my talents. I invested them, used them, took advantage of my opportunities, and many more were given to me in my seventeen months in the service.

As we walked to the open side of the ship, I was given two writing tablets, one a voucher register and the other an invoice ledger, along with two pencils. I was told how to check the tagging out, counting, and inspection of packed medicine, checking equipment in and filling out the invoices, as well as what to look for. I had a special section set up for me and two people were assigned to work with me. My tag read, Officer H BADGETT, which made me extremely proud. It meant that I was in charge, that I was a leader of men.

I met or saw all forty-two of the blacks on our ship; I was the only black soldier working as a clerk and not as a laborer. The eighteen whites working on this particular assignment were all clerks like me. I would say to this day that all of my fellow black soldiers seemed proud of me too, encouraged that one of their own had risen to officer status before their eyes.

We all took a forty-five-minute break for a snack in the mess hall and went back to work at 1330 hours. I might have a biased perspective, but I believe everyone in the group that caught my eyes, white and black, smiled at me that day. My group of personnel took a special pride in their work. We had everything tagged, counted, unloaded, packed, and loaded by 1550 hours. At that time, three officers came down to have a look. They prechecked the loaded and unloaded supplies, then called everyone together, thanked them, and announced an off day for all who had participated in the dock work. The group was thrilled.

We all went back to our units, the black soldiers to their lower levels, and when the officers were sure that everyone was out of hearing distance, they teased me one by one about how happy the group had been to work with me. Just before they let me go, they said that the group had enjoyed its assignment for the first time on that day. My chest swelled with pride again.

When I returned to my bunk, Richard, known as Rick, was there. We greeted each other, I undressed, showered, and relaxed in my pajamas afterward. I fell back on my bunk and commented, "I sure enjoyed the assignment today." Rick asked, "What can a

WHITE MAN'S TEARS CONQUER MY PAINS

person do on a troop ship that is that enjoyable?" I lay back on my crossed arms with my feet stretched out and crossed in front of me. I said, "For the first time in my life, I was part of a group that loaded and unloaded a supply ship delivery." I paused. Rick said, "Is that it?"

I replied, "No. There were eighteen white soldiers and me set up to count, tag, label, inspect, and vouch for all supplies delivered and returned, with forty-two black soldiers assigned to bring all parts, materials, medicines, equipment, and supplies from the warehouse on the dock, put it in storage on ship and bring all delivered products from the ship and put into storage in the warehouse. The assignment was completed in four hours, forty-five minutes. The joy of the job were the blacks, mostly young soldiers, who were really excited to see me as a clerk instead of as a laborer. Not a word was mentioned about this, yet every white person there was aware of my role and it was beautiful; it caused all of us to work harder and be more precise. To top the evening off, the officers in charge came and inspected the assignment, then thanked everyone and announced that a late dinner was being served and both detachments would be served as one."

Rick said, "Thanks for sharing that with me. That's the best news I have heard in about twenty months."

The races could work together and eat together; the barriers between us were manmade and ridiculous. My self-confidence in my leadership abilities also swelled that day.

Rick later asked me if I was going to the Philippines. I told him that I was. He said, "I have been in the Far East Command area since 1939, and this is my fourth assignment on this ship. My family was killed in a fire in 1937, and this is my comfort."

I asked, "Rick, what was one of your most memorable assignments during your tour of duty?"

He said, "Are you kidding?"

I said, "No, I'm not." Little did I know that I was going to get a college level education and unique, inside look on the war in Asia.

He paused for a few seconds, then replied, "I guess it was the struggle the United States had to regain the Philippines, because it was by far the U.S. Army's largest commitment to the Asian war. MacArthur's long campaign on New Guinea had never caught the imagination of the American public, as did the marines' battle for the Pacific atolls. The general's grandeur was more imposing than his forces. Until late 1944, he seldom controlled more than four divisions in the field, which in Europe is a mere corps command. His next campaign, however, would become the main event in America's conflict with Japan."

"More than four hundred thousand Japanese awaited the invaders. The Philippines represented a critical link on the sea route between Hirohito's Southeast Asian empire and the home islands. Tokyo believed that a confrontation there would offer its best chance to bloody the Americans, if not throw them back into the sea, before the decisive battle—a chorus reprised in all of Japan's war plans."

"The Japanese difficulty was that their scattered forces lacked mobility in the face of American air and naval superiority. MacArthur could choose where to make his landings. It would be hard for the defenders to swiftly shift large bodies in response. On a map, the Philippine Islands resemble a dense scattering of jigsaw pieces. Their combined mass is almost as large as Japan, with rich, luxuriant vegetation, and extravagant weather cycles. After the 1898 Spanish-American War, which ended European hegemony, U.S. Army representative from Texas, Carl Aims argued in Washington for the case against granting independence to Filipinos. He cited 'the divine law of human society, which makes us our brother's keeper. God has been preparing the English-speaking and Teutonic people to bring order out of chaos. He made us adept in government so that we might administer government among savage and senile people.'"

"Filipinos and U.S. representatives from General MacArthur's staff had a private meeting on a ship I was assigned to as water crafter Engineer. I had to be a part of the negotiating team, and that was the most interesting business meeting I had ever seen. Filipinos resisted U.S. dominance in the early days by violent insurgency and never ceased to crave independence. Socially, the islands were dominated by a rich landlord class. The mass of peasants remained poor and bitterly alienated from the plantation-type lords. Two-thirds of Filipinos between twenty and thirty-nine were uneducated, yet many Americans retained a romantic conviction that the virtue of their intentions made U.S. rule over the Philippines somehow more honorable than that of, say, the British in India. U.S. soldiers who served on the islands before 1942 regarded them as a leisure resort, offering cheap comforts, servants, and amenities of a kind they never knew back home, amidst a lazy Spanish culture.

"Japan's thirty-month-old occupation had been patchy in its impact: oppressive and brutal in some places—in the most strategically important places, naturally, including the capital, Manila—while scarcely felt in remote areas. In 1943, the Japanese granted the Philippines, along with most of their other occupied territories, self-government under a local puppet regime. Yet such was the mindless cruelty of Tokyo's soldiers that this gesture inspired little gratitude among Filipinos. Imperial General HQ reported in March 1944: 'Even after their independence, there remains among all classes a strong undercurrent of pro-American sentiment. Guerilla activities are gradually increasing.' The Japanese fully controlled only twelve of the country's eighteen provinces. Elsewhere, guerilla bands roamed widely, American-armed and sometimes American-led. Several U.S. officers, such as the legendary Richard Sims, had survived in the hills of Luzon since the spring of 1942. Others merely pursued lives of banditry."

Rick looked at the time. It was 0215 hours. He said, "I had no idea it was this late."

I said, "It's okay. I am off for the rest of the week anyway."

Rick replied, "This was a fine visit," and he turned his lights off and said, "Good night, mate."

CHAPTER EIGHT

Docking at Wake Island

I woke up at 0525 hours, and we were in the middle of the Pacific Ocean, with no land in sight. When I went to breakfast, I found out we would be docking at Wake Island around 1600 hours. We eventually docked there at 1840 hours. It was a small island with very few people, and it was very quiet. There were quite a few U.S. soldiers, about twelve to fifteen of whom were black, from what I saw. Rick and I had breakfast together, the first time I had shared breakfast with a friend since joining the army. He and I actually had interesting subjects to discuss.

After we finished eating, Rick said, "Our cabinmate, Ted, and I talked about you, and he said he thought you were with a special personnel unit."

I answered, "Did he?" I paused and then said, "I know you and Ted are friends."

We both laughed and got up and went back to the cabin, where I finished packing and he got ready for duty. We shook hands and he left. He made me feel like a real man.

Rick knew I was indeed assigned to a special unit, and that is why he had taught me how to operate a field radio—he had been instructed to do so. But neither he nor I knew exactly which unit I was being trained for. It was only right before I began to carry out my duties in the Philippines that I knew I was being developed into a leader of the elite Tracker team.

We unloaded supplies, equipment, and a few other items. We left a few personnel and picked up a few. We had dinner, and I went back to my bunk to read a book. I went to sleep early, around 2100 hours, but soon after, the loudspeaker announced that all personnel had to prepare for safety procedures, I promptly got up. All the lights were out, but I could tell the motors had picked up speed. Everything else was quiet.

About 2300 hours, we heard four or five planes flying very low. I assumed they were U.S. planes because there were no Japanese planes supposed to be flying. There were Japanese submarines still patrolling the Pacific because their crews either did not know the war was over, due to their base of communications having been destroyed, or their officers refused to surrender to the U.S. Surrender for those officers would mean either prison for life or death; neither option appealed to them. For those sub crews, the war was still on, and they were eager to sink U.S. ships like ours.

At 0435 hours, the loudspeaker called off the alert. At 0610, the announcement came over telling us that the breakfast menu had been changed. We could have coffee, milk, cocoa, and toast, or K rations but not both. The mess hall was open, as usual.

At 0940 hours that day, the loudspeaker told us that we were in the waters near the Mariana Islands, and that our next docking should be on Guam Island. I was lying in my bunk when Ted came into the cabin and said, "This has been a hell of a shift."

I replied, "This just goes to prove that anywhere you go, a good man is hard to find, and you are no exception."

Ted asked, "What are you saying?"

"I'm saying that in cases when things happen like what happens on this ship, there is very little rest for a person with a solid extent of engineering talent, and you and Rick have that talent."

"Rick told me about you and he had a nice conversation."

"Yes, we did. He's quite an interesting person. Are you and him the same classified type of engineer?"

"You could say we handle some of the same problems. We are in the same area working sometimes, but we don't have our residing quarters in the same location. My responsibilities deal mostly with electronics, and he deals with watercraft." He smiled. "We keep this lady dancing."

"That must be interesting."

"Fun sometimes, hell sometimes, just like a woman. Like the last fourteen hours, she's been busy being smart."

He lay back with his head in his hands, crossed his legs, and we didn't talk for a few minutes. He smiled, got up, and announced, "I think I'll have a toddy." He offered me a drink of rum. I declined.

He sat down on the bunk and asked, "Henry, what part are you playing in this great recapture of the Philippines Islands?"

I laughed and thought, *Is he trying to find out who I am and why I am asking so many questions? Does he think I am an officer? Why can't I socialize with whites and reside in officers' quarters?*

I looked him straight in the eye and said, "Do you remember when the president called General MacArthur back to the United States and MacArthur said, 'I shall return'?"

"Yes," Ted answered.

I smiled and said, "He just lied; he's sending me instead."

He thought about it for a minute and we shared a good laugh. Then I said, "I really don't know what the army will do with me, and I won't know until I get my assignment in the Philippines. I was told I would be dropped off in Quezon Province. After that, who knows?"

He looked at me and said, "Henry, you are smart enough to do good anywhere you go."

"Thanks," I said.

I lay there awhile, then he said, "What do you call home?"

"Dallas."

He jumped up. "You are kidding!"

"I went to Lincoln High School."

He responded, "I went to Booker T. Washington in north Dallas. I grew up on a farm in east Texas, in a little town called Paris. I'm from a family of seven, and I picked cotton from age five or six and up. After school on weekends, whenever I got the time, we played sandlot football. In high school, when we practiced or played football, we played in the afternoons because we didn't have a lighted field. I played both sides of the field, defensive end, and cornerback. I tried kicking field goals, but I was terrible."

"I played everything that was a challenge, from marbles to baseball, football, basketball, wrestling, soldiers fighting, and skate racing in the paved streets. When we played basketball, we played at night. The bus stopped running early after we stopped playing. Some of the fellows would walk about six miles home. If my mother was home, that was cool because she was there most of the time, but if my old man was there and had had a few drinks, he would bitch as long as I was in his company. My senior year, the team voted me captain of the football team. That meant a lot to me because it came from the players. Lord knows, I wasn't a big kid. I weighed about 140 pounds, but I was fast and I could hit hard."

"I wanted to go to college, but I didn't have two quarters to rub together, so going to college was not something I could do. When Pearl Harbor hit, I was working in Dallas and living with my sister. I got a job as a traveling salesman for Padget Leather

& Rubber Company, selling leather clothes and women's shoes' heels, men's boots, women's boots, and many other products from a magazine. I sold to wholesale stores and retail establishments."

"There was a general expectation throughout the country that all young men would do their duty and enlist. People I met on the road often asked me why I wasn't in uniform. No matter what day, I would always say, 'As soon as some documents come back from the board of education.' That became my standard answer. One day I met a fellow and he told me that if I finished high school and could pass a special army exam, he thought he could get me into a training school to become a warrant officer. After some time served, I could become a second lieutenant in the Marine Corps. Sure enough, I passed the test and went to training for eight months and became a warrant officer for eight months. I then went to a tech school, got into electronics, and got most of my experience from on-the-job training."

He paused for a few minutes. I said, "When did you get promoted to first lieutenant?"

"February 1945. Rick outranks me by two years. He should make captain in the next sixty to ninety days. He was already recommended and approved."

"Great for him."

"It almost slipped my mind. I should meet with a mate I work with. Excuse me."

"Sure."

Surely one of the most unusual aspects for many of us who served in World War II was to end up halfway around the world in close quarters with people whom we have never met, yet hailed from nearly the same neighborhood. What are the chances of me rooming with another man from Dallas? It was just another way that I felt more at home every day on that ship and in the army.

To this day, I count it a true privilege to have spent time with my esteemed bunkmates. I was an eighteen-year-old kid, nothing more, yet these two men consistently treated me with respect and passed on some valuable training. I worshipped the ground they walked on, and they thought highly of me as well. My weeks with these men were priceless as I weigh my life experiences, a truly unforgettable period in my life.

CHAPTER NINE

Service in Guam

I looked out the porthole on our twenty-second day at sea and realized that we had left the dock and we're on our way up the Mariana waters to Guam, my first real assigned station. It was 2235 hours. I wondered what time we had left the dock. I had looked out the porthole about 1750 hours and I believed that we were still docked. I figured I would take a shower and then finish the book I was reading.

While I was in the shower, the loudspeaker announced that we were off course and headed to the southeast waters of the Pacific. As a result, all lights and appliances would be turned off until further notice. Assigned mates were to return to their stations. Little did I know that our ship had suddenly become the bait to lure a Japanese submarine to its demise.

At 0515 hours, the ship announcer came on and said that the mess hall would not open that morning, and that K rations would be issued to all personnel that needed that day's rations.

WHITE MAN'S TEARS CONQUER MY PAINS

The rations to be issued consisted of oatmeal, rolls, bacon, coffee, or milk at door 041 in the mess hall, open from 0600-0645 hours. All docks were off limits until further notice.

I picked up my scrumptious breakfast and headed back to my cabin. I read, played cards, and went back to the mess hall and picked up some potato soup and a beef sandwich (K-ration style), plus some lemonade. I robbed Snickers, crackers, Coca-cola, and peanut butter from Ted, whom I had not seen since 1315 hours the day before. I figured that if I had to choose between dying of starvation and being thrown into jail for theft, I would choose jail because the food was good. I had forgotten that the kitchen was closed, and realized that if the mess hall was closed long term, I could be on the verge of my hardest time in the service.

I did some exercising and went to bed. The ship announcer woke me up at 0515 hours and let the personnel on the ship know that K-rations were being served for breakfast again. The mess hall was closed. All docks were again off limits and all appliances were turned off. I wasn't sure if I could take another day without being in someone's company. Thankfully, Ted came to the cabin at around 1915 hours.

I said, "I hope you won't miss some of your snacks. I just couldn't resist them when the choice was K-rations or snacks."

Ted laughed and said, "That is why I keep an extra stock of snacks." He reached under his bunk and got the neatest little lantern and took a shower with it. He said, "You are free to use this when you need to."

I asked, "Did you see Rick?"

Ted said, "Yes. He assigned me to about seven different jobs. I hope to learn about 50 percent of his talent."

"Really?"

"Yes. He is smart and highly respected in the hole."

Ted and I talked for about an hour and a half and he went back to work. It was a great visit, and I went right to sleep. The ship announcer again woke everyone up at 0515 with the same message for the third straight day. At 1110 hours, he announced that the mess hall would be serving hot meals starting at 1130 and 1215 hours. He also said that all docks were open and that all appliances could be used as desired. He added that we would be passing the city of Leyte, but that we would not dock.

The ship docked in Guam. It had taken us twenty-nine days to make what was usually a nine-day trip, but I was not complaining. That voyage at sea was worth every minute to me.

I got all of my belongings together and disembarked from the ship. I walked over to a military station and inquired about the personnel who would be picking me up. I was told that I should have transportation shortly, so I just sat and relaxed. I looked back at the ship that I had been on, and I saw many white and black soldiers unloading from the ship. Some entered the military station; some were picked up in trucks. Some gathered in groups and other men boarded the ship I had been on.

I saw a soldier come up to two or three military people, and then he came over to me and asked if I was Private Badgett. I replied, "Yes, I am." He said, "Follow me, please," and we went to a carrier vehicle, where he helped me load my belongings. We exchanged introductions.

"I'm Corporal Wallace O'Neal. The group calls me Wally. I'm assigned to the bakery. Are you assigned to the 151 QM Bakery?"

I replied, "That is what my assignment papers say."

He looked at me and smiled. "This should be fun."

"What do you mean?"

"We are an all-white unit."

"That's okay with me, if you can handle it."

"I most certainly can."

We both laughed.

We were passing an air base and I asked what base is this? Wally replied that it was the Andersen Air Base. I asked, "U.S.?" He said, "Yes." He then asked me if I answered to a shorter name, such as Hank. I said, "Sure."

He said, "I do not only answer to Wally, but I like Wally. I really hope you are coming to be a part of our group."

"That would be a nice change. Believe it or not, I was in Detachment One coming over, but I think the training camp got my records mixed up. I have had a great time with the situation, but I have a feeling things will change. Let's face it—why would the army change this situation just for me?"

Wally looked at me and said, "Because you're cool."

"Not that cool," I replied.

Wally thought for a few minutes and replied, "Maybe they are using you, and if you work out, maybe they will extend it into a program, with all soldiers living together. We are fighting together."

I looked at Wally and said, "Let's keep dreaming."

Wally looked up and said, "We are home. Now let the fun begin."

We went into the office headquarters and met a Sergeant William Scott, and we introduced ourselves to each other. I turned my necessary papers over to the sergeant and he ordered Wally to take me to the barrack and help me unpack my belongings. He also asked me to return to his office as soon as I had finished unpacking. After we unpacked I went back to the office and he explained my assignment. He let me know that it was a special assignment and I was to meet a group of soldiers, but their assignment was delayed and I would be assigned for duties there at the bakery until the soldiers arrived. In the meantime, I would be assigned to Barrack G for three days. A special barrack was built and furnished for fifteen personnel at Andersen, and I remained in that barrack until the group of soldiers returned from their assignment. I thanked Sgt. Scott and later learned that I was assigned to the kitchen; my duties were "as needed."

I remained at the bakery for about two months, living in Barrack G, and cleaned pots, pans, and equipment, as well as stocking supplies and doing maintenance. I was a regular utility person, and the men were very nice and fair with me. Only one person wanted an Uncle Tom for a fellow soldier, and he was the dumbest person in the company. His name was Michael, but he was known as Mad Man. One day I asked him to have a break with me. He said okay, so we met. The first thing he had asked me before we were introduced was, "What the hell are you doing here?" I said, "Sit your ass down and let's pretend we really like each other." He sat on a big product can. I continued, "My name is Henry. What is your name?"

"They call me Mad Man."

In a strong voice, I repeated, "What the hell is your name?"

"Michael. Why do you want to know?"

"I just want you to know I don't have time to hate you. Shit, I am busy hating Japanese. Do you hate me?"

"No."

Before he could say anything else, I wrapped my arms around him and said, "Good, Michael. We are going to kick some Japanese ass, okay?" I stood up and said, "Let me get back to work."

From that day on, we interacted every day, even if we had to just wave to each other.

The soldiers that had been on assignment finally returned to Andersen, and a Sergeant and I went to the dock and picked them up: fourteen young black soldiers. We took them to the barracks and then met with the head sergeant of the 151 QM Bakery. He told us that we were to meet with a special group of people at 2000 hour the same night they had arrived. I enjoyed my time in the bakery, but I had a feeling that I had not been shipped halfway around the world, trained in how to use a field radio, and instructed in jungle survival to simply make biscuits for soldiers. My hunch was soon proven correct.

The army wasted no time preparing us for special training. We met before we could get too acquainted with each other, but that was all right; it was important that we knew that we were there for each other. That was all we needed to build on.

We met for two hours the first day and started our field training, which lasted five weeks and changed me completely. My group and I were furnished living quarters that consisted of regular army double-frame beds, trunks that fit under the beds, dressers on each side, hangers on the walls, and two desks in the front of the barrack. We were told that meals would be served at the mess hall on base. Training schedules would be posted in the barracks if necessary. Lunch was served at 1230 hours on that day for Barrack 15, and a meeting was set for 1500 hours.

We got together and were advised of our first assignment and our future responsibilities, as well as the personnel we would take our immediate orders from. We then were told that we would be off duty until 0630 the next day, when breakfast would be served, followed by training at 0730.

In no time at all, our training got very specific—and it was not on the proper way to clean an oven. My men and I spent five weeks learning special jungle training, learning how to engage the enemy in hand-to-hand combat, how to use radio signals when in the field, and other principles of jungle warfare, which are completely different than tactics used in other contexts of war. One aspect of this training that I will never forget was our use of only the initials in our names as we communicated. We never did learn each other's first and last names, let alone talk about private matters of any kind. I was called Mr. HB, which had a nice ring to it.

At the time, we did not know why we were taught certain procedures, but we gave it our all just the same, knowing that if we ever did use this training in actual engagement with the enemy, our lives would be on the line. In war, that means that you not only take care of yourself, but you look out for everyone around you. That would be primarily my job, as the Unit leader.

After the training, I spent one day in Guam, then was shipped to Quezon Province, the Philippines, by boat. I'm not sure if that boat was government-owned or private. The rest of the group was shipped out later, and I helped to pick them up two or three days after I arrived in Quezon Province.

CHAPTER TEN

First Assignment in the Philippines

When I arrived at the dock in Quezon Province, a carrier was waiting for me. The driver was a sergeant named Steve Spencer. Sgt. Spencer delivered me straight to the office of the company. He helped me get my belongings off the carrier truck and said, "I bet the sergeant will be surprised." Sure enough, when he looked up, the expression on the sergeant's face, Master Sgt. Walter Bronson, let us know that he was surprised. He looked at me and said, "Do you have the right papers?"

I said, "Can't you tell?" and he, Steve, and me just started laughing. I felt that we were at least getting off on the right foot in a situation that would have to be resolved. In the meantime, I was introduced to the immediate crew in the office. After MSgt.

Bronson finished the introductions, he asked me if I was hungry. I said, "I can wait until dinner at the mess hall."

He looked at Sgt. Spencer and said, "Get him a bunk." Sgt. Spencer said, "Yes, sir," then said to me, "You don't know what the hell you are starting."

I looked at him and said, "You don't have to worry about that. We can handle that problem when we come to it, can't we?" I smiled.

Sgt. Spencer said, "What the hell are you laughing about?"

I replied, "You and I had better start finding a way to fight those bad-ass Japanese and pick up hating each other when we get back home. Shit, we can't fight each other and those Japanese too." I looked at him and smiled. Again, he looked at me and gave me a half-smile.

I said, "That was a pretty good smile you just gave me, not too bad for a first smile to a new friend."

We got to the barrack as we both carried my belongings. When we walked in, there were about a dozen soldiers there. I stopped Sgt. Spencer at the front of the barrack and said, "Steve, do me a favor, please."

"What?"

"I would like you to introduce me to each person in the barrack now. Just as you pass the bunk, say as an example, 'John, this is HB.' 'Tom, this is HB,' and so on, okay?"

"I guess I can do that."

"Thanks, pal."

There were several guys who wanted to know what was going on, why a black soldier was moving into an all-white barrack. I said, "Anybody who wants to know more about what is going on is welcome to come to my bunk when I get unpacked."

When we got to the bunk that Steve said was assigned to me, it was an upper bunk. I asked, "Why are you giving me this bunk?"

He said, "The lower bunk available is next to a person I don't think you would like."

I said, "Let he and I decide that."

He looked at me and said, "I'm betting on you."

After Steve helped me finish unpacking, we sat and got more acquainted. He told me he was from Atlanta, Georgia, and that he was raised on a farm. He had two sisters and one older brother who was in jail for twelve to twenty years for several crazy things and had been there since 1937. He said he had been following in his brother's footsteps when a schoolteacher, Jesse Pierce, came to his home one day after Steve had gotten out of a juvenile house of corrections.

"He visited with me for about four hours," Steve recounted. "He talked to me about my life and future. He said that if I was really interested in making something out of my life, he would try everything he could to help me start a new life. He convinced me that I really needed his help. Mr. Pierce called up about three days after his visit and told me to meet him at school at 1130 on Monday morning. I got cleaned up. I put on a pair of blue jeans that was like new and met him. He had a soldier there and they both talked to me about going into the service. They knew about my run-in with the law. They gave me some papers for my parents to fill out, and they showed me how to help them fill those out. I took the papers home to my parents and they were so proud. We filled the papers out and celebrated like we had never celebrated before."

"My girlfriend had wanted to get married before I left, but I wouldn't do that because I made my insurance policy out to my family. I enlisted in the service in 1943. I was nineteen years old. It was the best thing that had ever happened to me."

I said, "That's a beautiful story. How long have you been in the Philippines?"

"Since 1945," he answered. "Before that, I trained recruits at Fort Benning, Georgia."

"Sergeant, that was a great decision you made and I am very proud to have met you." I added on a completely different topic, "What time does the mess hall open for dinner?" He told me 1800 hours until 2000 hours. I looked at him and said, "It's 1425 hours. Do you think I should talk with the guys here in the barrack?"

"If you'd like," he replied. "But please let me talk with them first. MSgt. Bronson asked that you return and see him in a couple of hours concerning your papers. That was at about 1135 hours."

I said, "Thanks, Steve. That had skipped my mind. I'll take care of that right now."

I went to MSgt. Bronson's office and he smiled and said, "Come in and have a seat. Sergeant said the troop ship you were on led a Japanese submarine into a trap and it was captured at 0335 hours two days ago, 230 kilometers from Guam. The traitors, three of them, overpowered the submarine and it had to submerge with thirty-five sailors without a shot. That was the first captured submarine in these waters since 1943, when it took almost ten hours—and that submarine had been heavily damaged. We had a meeting and I was told the air base would have lodging for you and a group. The group will report to the station at 0900 tomorrow." I said, "Okay."

It turns out that I spent only three days in the barrack with an all-white group of soldiers. My new barrack was for black soldiers and could hold fifteen. A few days later, the other fourteen black soldiers arrived in Quezon, joining me in Barrack 15.

I could see that my radio training, given to me courtesy of my two bunkmates on the ship, would come in handy too. I also began to discern how I had been prepared all along for my assignment, from the time I had spent living in white units on the ship to living with the white unit at the 151 QM Bakery. I, now was part of the seventy-sixth white squad in Quezon Province.

After my unit had trained together for a few days, all of a sudden we were called in for a briefing on a special assignment: to secretly go as a group of seven and locate a wrecked airliner plane that had crashed in the past three or four hours in the jungle, about fifteen to twenty-five miles between Quezon City and Manila. I remember the weather that day as being very wet as it poured down rain, which undoubtedly contributed to the accident. The plane was a private jet, and we were tasked with locating the wreckage, verifying the identity of as many passengers as possible and taking photos if possible. Sergeant Steve took us to a location near the wreckage area and instructed us on how to get in touch with him when we wanted to return.

I requested, "Why don't you stay close for about fifteen minutes? I mean, just drive slow or to that little town we passed through about ten minutes ago." I was thinking of the information we had been given about Japanese soldiers living in the trees deep in the jungle, all over the island. In case we needed to make a quick getaway, I wanted a plan B. Sergeant Steve did not see it my way.

We were dropped off and crept into the jungle for about thirty minutes. Then—we could see the wreckage. As we surveyed the area, we could see things moving around under the wreckage in the front of the plane. I signaled the others to cover and wait for me as I got a closer view of the wreck. I moved in behind the wreckage and identified the moving things as Japanese soldiers going through the debris and examining dead passengers.

I then moved back to a place where I could communicate with my colleagues and told them that there were Japanese soldiers at the wreckage rifling through people's clothing. I told them, "Prepare to fight and shoot to kill." We surrounded the wreckage and shot four Japanese soldiers. I picked off, two myself. We checked the area closely to make sure that no other enemy soldiers were around. We then took photos of several passengers who still had recognizable faces, confiscated briefcases, searched the area thoroughly, and determined that all passengers were indeed dead.

As we exited the wreckage, we saw military and other people approaching the location of the downed jet. We called for transportation from the air base and were picked up in about twenty-five minutes at the specified location. We loaded into the truck and after going about four or five blocks, one of the men (TT) said that we were short one person. "Where is LS?" he asked. I had to tell him that LS had not made it. TT then got up from his seat and said, "Let's go back and get him!" I had to explain more clearly: "I checked and he didn't make it." He then looked me straight in the eyes and said, "Listen, punk, you are still wet behind the ears. How can you make a decision on a thing like that?"

The driver, Sgt. Spencer, pulled the truck over and turned around in his seat. "Listen, soldier," he said, "Mr. HB is in charge of this assignment, and one more word out of your ass and we will see where you end up as soon as we get back to the base. Do you understand, soldier?"

"Yes, sir," he replied.

Sgt. Spencer said, "I can't hear you."

In a louder tone, the soldier said, "Yes, sir."

Sgt. Spencer turned back around and dropped a heavy canopy plaster that was used as a window to cut off the sound between the cab and the rest of the truck. We drove for a few minutes and he asked, "What happened at the plane site?"

I told him, "I will not discuss that with you. I will make a report of the assignment."

He then asked, "What's in those briefcases?"

I answered. "Sergeant, that will be made public when I turn them over to MSgt. Bronson." I later learned that there was a $10 million reward for one of the briefcases. Sgt. Spencer looked desperate. I looked at him and said, "I am ashamed of you. I thought you were my strength."

We got closer to the base and Sgt. Spencer said, "What the hell is going on?" There were about ten or fifteen Filipino officers waiting for us at a roadblock. One asked Sgt. Spencer what his assignment was. He replied, "Sir, U.S. Government, sir." The officer said, "As you were, sir."

He moved to the next vehicle and we were soon out of the jam. After about another twenty minutes of driving, Sgt. Spencer looked at me and said, "You are making a damn good soldier.

WHITE MAN'S TEARS CONQUER MY PAINS

Keep up the personality. It is heavy stuff." He obviously liked my style as a soldier, which I will humbly admit was the predominant attitude taken by all officers who had contact with me, no matter what color they were.

I said, "Thanks. People like you make it fun."

Sgt. Spencer said, "I sure hope we get better acquainted in the future."

"I'll be surprised if our group is at this base more than seventy-two hours from today."

"Do you know something I don't?"

"Yes. When it concerns my assignments, something I really don't know much about."

"I don't think Master Sergeant would have made this big move if his intentions weren't to have you and the group for awhile. Let's wait and see."

We turned in to the base and the soldiers seemed to be waiting for us. They came right out and immediately started to unload personnel. They also took the briefcases inside and gave them to MSgt. Bronson. Sgt. Spencer asked me to remain there and I said, "Yes, sir."

Eventually, we went in to the office and MSgt. Bronson said, "Thanks, Pvt. HB. You and the crew did a hell of a job. Too bad we lost a soldier."

I said, "Yes, the assignment was close, Sergeant," alerting him that a whole crowd of military and civilian personnel had shown up so close to our investigation site.

MSgt. Bronson said, "You realize that you and the group will have to vanish for awhile."

"Yes, sir, I do."

"Will you give me the briefing on the results?"

"Yes, sir, plus documented paperwork."

"Thanks."

I went to the barracks. The soldier (TT) with whom I had exchanged tense words in the truck apologized to me and I accepted his apology. About fifteen minutes later, Sgt. Spencer came in and said that dinner would be served in twenty minutes. We thanked him for the notice.

After dinner, the group went back to the barracks and talked about our reason for needing to disappear for awhile and what our assignments were really all about. I told them the truth about the air force wanting the credit for getting the information from the plane, and that the government probably didn't know we were assigned to this job, but we still had to be committed to doing the very best job that we could. "I don't know where we will be going next," I said, "but I think it will be fun, so just relax and have a good evening. We are a team." We were an invisible team, a team that would not be glorified, a team that would work in the shadows and put its collective life on the line, while the air force claimed that they had no idea we were around.

Even though I turned in all of the documents and pictures taken at the wreckage, which provided valuable intelligence to my superiors, it was as if we were dispensable and my men I had never crept into the jungle. It takes a certain attitude to carry out such a mission, in the military or in life, for that matter. For us, it helped to know that we were entrusted with an ultra-secret mission. That enabled us to balance the realization that we would never, ever be acknowledged by the public or even other members of the military. We were a true stealth unit, highly trained for an intensely specific mission. This first success was just a warm-up for adventures to follow.

We shared breakfast the next morning and later had lunch together. MSgt. Bronson came in while we were eating lunch and told me he wanted me to report to his office at 1430 hours. I went to his office as requested and he closed the door. He said, "That was a very good report you left on my desk."

I replied, "Master Sergeant Bronson, it would be an honor if you would come to our barrack and say what you feel about the assignment we just completed. We are saddened with losing a member, and a personal comment from you would be greatly appreciated."

WHITE MAN'S TEARS CONQUER MY PAINS

Later, Msgt. Bronson did visit Barrack 15 and said, "Fellows, I am here to let you know how proud I was for the job you did on the last assignment and the entire country is proud. Thank you."

During another visit in his office, MSgt. Bronson had a dilemma handed to him that I helped him to solve. As we were relaxing and chatting about what to call each other (he had asked me what to call me in private, and I had said, "How about, HB? Thanks."), a sergeant knocked and came in. MSgt. Bronson got up and asked, "How can I help you, Sergeant?" The sergeant said, "This is a private matter." MSgt. Bronson then asked me, "HB, will you please excuse me for a few minutes?" I said, "Yes, sir," and they left the office.

Sgt. Bronson returned in a few minutes. He sat back in his chair with his arms stretched behind his head. He looked up slowly and said, "The Filipino officers, U.S. government, U.S. Army personnel, and news members are accusing a U.S. black soldier that was found at the wreckage of a plane as a terrorist. Somebody has to get the message to the right source that the soldier was a member of a special group, The Trackers. This group was assigned to investigate the plane to check if there were Americans, Japanese, Chinese, or other groups that can be terrorists on board. The group returned with personal briefcases from the plane wreckage and pictures. This group was organized to track dropped supply and/or medicine from U.S. planes that we try and recover. In this case we were looking for spies, Japanese, Americans, Chinese, or other terrorists or something we could use."

MSgt. Bronson got up and went into another office and told the personnel not to let anyone into his office. I said, "Sgt. Bronson, I suggest you find out who the main person is to discuss this situation with. Invite this person and two others to meet with you. Show them the briefcases, pictures, and my report. Tell them we have moved to another location and you cannot disclose the location. You should not go any further with this problem."

MSgt. Bronson said, "Henry, I recommended you for a field ranking. I'm not sure what will happen, since you have been in service less than six months, but if it is approved, it will be T/S (Tech Sergeant). Don't hold your breath."

"Thank you, sir," I said.

The phone rang and MSgt. Bronson said hello. He talked about one minute and ended with okay. He hung up the phone, looked at me, and said, "A carrier will pick the group up in thirty minutes for Baguio."

I would go to my next mission as a Tech Sergeant, leading LS, DG, BM, JT, CL, WJ, HH, MR, PA, EK, AN, TT, SP, and KS, each set of initials representing a brave warrior, a true man, a military hero willing to give his all to his country. Before we would find out if that were necessary, we spent about two weeks in a place that was very close to paradise, particularly for several of the men in my group.

How deep of an impact did these men make on me, these men under my care? I can still recite most of their initials from memory, a full sixty-eight years after I led them in battle. I found an official government document in the Department of Veterans Affairs about two decades ago that listed all of the initials of my special bunch. I was the one they called Mr., Mr. HB to be exact.

CHAPTER ELEVEN

Baguio

We landed in Baguio City in the afternoon and were signed in with no problems. We had a meeting in my room and went our way until later that evening. I unloaded my clothes and other items and relaxed. We went to dinner and had a wonderful evening. After dinner, we went out on a patio and all had a drink. Mine was non-alcoholic, but I don't know what the others had. There was another U.S. serviceman there that kept an eye on us.

The entertainment started at 2030 hours, and within about fifteen minutes, ten to fifteen women came in alone. A little later, we all had refills and the waiter said, "You gentlemen can ask the single ladies to dance or whatever." We thanked him, and before the evening was over we had the ladies join us. We had a great time together.

The next morning we met for breakfast and the guys could not stop talking about the fun that they had enjoyed the previous evening. They thanked me profusely for going all out and letting them party. I sat watching them and thought: *These may be the last days of our lives, after what happened on the last assignment. Maybe that is why our voucher said Unlimited Purchases, ten thousand dollars cash. Must use voucher number for more than $1,000 cash per order.*

The other members of the group did not know the voucher's value. We stayed at the Baguio resort about twelve days. We had access to boating, dinners on a boat, hiking, swimming, golf, horseback riding, private movies, and machine games, all of which kept us amused.

But, of course, the prime attraction and primary source of amusement were the women, who were readily available for a price. I remember looking at HH, someone who never had much to say, sitting with a stunning young lady that he had spent the previous night with, the couple as happy as they could be. It had started a little rough, with HH asking me how much cash he could have and if he would have to pay it back. I looked at him quizzically and asked just how much he would need. He responded, "$200." I reached into my pocket and produced four $50 bills. Just after his face lit up like a Christmas tree, he dropped his head and admitted, "I am a virgin. What should I do?"

I replied, "Use a condom each time."

"Do you have condoms?"

"No."

"How do I ask for them?"

"Wait right here." I went and got him a small package for free.

Just then, TT came and said, "Boss, can I get a little advance cash?"

I replied, "My name is not Boss."

He wiped the smile off his face and said, "I'm sorry, Mr. HB. Can I borrow some cash?"

"How much?"

The same figure for the same purpose: "$200."

I again reached into my pocket and produced the bills. He said, "Thank you, sir."

I quickly asked, "TT, do you have a condom?"

"Sure do."

"Fine."

By this time it was getting late, around midnight. I went to the desk and got $200 each for the other guys. One lady had not partnered up with anyone else. I asked her if she would join me, and she said, "Yes." We had a perfect evening, enjoying a snack and a drink, talking openly about how pleasant the night was. She realized I was the go-to guy for birth control as three or four men came to me and asked for condoms.

She asked, "Why is it when I look at your face with that young, beautiful smile, I see that trusting look of confidence that you show, and when these fellows come to you for guidance, you have the answer that they want? Then, when you look at me, you have the answer to everything I would like to know about Mr. HB?"

"We all need someone we can trust," I humbly replied.

Later, I calculated just how much some of those ladies made at $200 per service. Many of them had eight or nine rendezvous with my men. That's a wad of money, all paid for by the U.S. government.

The sexual escapades got a little crazy at times. After a long round of drinking and game playing one night, four of my guys decided to swap women. TT had hatched the idea because he wanted SP's girl. SP responded by saying that he was perfectly happy with his choice, and his woman echoed that sentiment. TT countered with, "I am not saying I don't want this nice lady that I'm with. I'm saying that we are strong enough to swap and not be afraid that you are not enough man for your woman." He looked right at SP when he said that. SP looked at his woman and asked if she could handle the change. She said, "Yes, I'm with the party."

Right after that, it got very quiet for awhile as men and women suddenly found themselves with new partners. Eventually, several couples took to the dance floor. After a few minutes, TT, the biggest soldier in that group, asked to switch partners. SP accepted the change, as did other members of the group. The woman who had been with SP and were now with TT left the room first, followed by SP's new partner. Ten minutes later, SP's new girl hollered, "Oh my! Oh my!" She ran into where TT was getting busy with SP's former lover and she kissed TT on the head, saying memorably, "Thank you! Thank you!" SP eventually emerged from his room in his birthday suit and asked what was wrong. It was apparent that he had twice as much tool to work with as TT, and the whole party laughed uproariously at TT's expense. He was so embarrassed that he left the premises, but his first partner followed soon after and convinced him that she was the one who was embarrassed because he had not been satisfied with her. She added that she liked him before they had engaged in sex, and that sex alone didn't make a good man or a good lover. She went on to report that she and SP had not had intercourse, that he had told her that intercourse alone did not make people true lovers.

I remember all of this because I had asked my girl to keep a record of what happened that night. The four men who came to me for condoms also asked for advice on problems they were having with their partners for the two weeks. My woman and I did our best to help them. The questions ranged from BM asking how to ask a lady to teach him how to kiss her between her legs to JT asking how to request a lady to give him head. My answer to the first query was, "Prepare her for the attempt by first playing with her stomach. From there on, it's up to you."

As for the second question, my girl advised, "Just ask her, and accept yes or no as an answer."

Another query from DG involved the proper way to ask a woman for sex in the butt. He was told, "Find a special and sexy way to let her know what you want, and then accept yes or no as the answer."

KS wanted to know if you had to ask a lady before sucking on her breast. He was told to simply "act experienced."

At another point during our time in Baguio, AN and EK came to me and asked if they could talk with me in private. I said, "Sure, why not?" We went into another room and they both admitted that they were virgins. One of them said he didn't think he was gay, and the other said that he had not experienced either form of sex, so he was not sure what he was. They asked earnestly, "What should we do with the girls?" They did not want the other guys to know about their "problem."

I responded, "Guys, you have a serious problem. My lady friend in the other room is very smart. Why don't we ask her and see what happens? We will never see her again anyway. What do you say?"

"Okay," they replied.

"All right, let me start with the questions."

We went into the other room, where my partner was.

"Hello, pretty lady. We have some questions for you. I have two guys here that are virgins. One is not sure if he is gay or not. Can you help us?"

She asked AN, "Did you ever look at a girl and get a hard-on just thinking of what could happen? Just thinking about her being naked?"

AN responded, "Yes. I had that happen when I looked at a couple of girls when I was drinking."

My friend asked EK the same questions. He replied, "Yes."

She continued, "Have you ever played with yourself when thinking about sex? Were you thinking about another boy?"

EK said quickly, "No."

My friend asked, "Were you thinking about a girl?"

"Yes," EK said.

She looked at AN and said, "How about you?"

He also said, "Yes, I was thinking about a girl."

My new friend suggested a radical plan, "Because you and your friend know about each other, why don't you have a naked party with your girls? Have a few drinks and play a game where you will end up naked. Then, let whatever happens happen."

The two men did as suggested, and the four in that party remained inseparable during our entire time in Baguio. Every time AN or EK saw my friend they came over to her and greeted her warmly.

One day, PA was coming from the office and saw one of the members of the personnel at the resort. The person asked, "How are things going?" PA responded, "The morning came too soon. We really didn't want yesterday and last night to end, but some things you just can't control."

He continued as he shared our latest idea for fun, "Mr. HB said he spoke with a person that offered our group a chance to attend a boat dinner party. Our lady friends are supposed to let us know how many of them would like to attend. We will have a meeting at 1430 today for a decision. My lady friend says she would love to go." We did all meet at 1430, and all of the ladies were there. Everyone agreed that a boat dinner party would be a lot of fun. HH, PA, WJ, and their lady friends asked if they could go for a walk and meet everybody at the boat dock at 1830.

We met at the dock at the appointed time and were ushered to a nice table for twenty-eight people, even though there were only twenty-two of us. I had called the Baguio office about the party of six that had not shown up to complete our group, but no one knew its whereabouts. The boat left the dock at 1840. The announcer began by saying, "We intend to give everybody a great evening of good food, entertainment, drinks, and a hangover if you are not careful. Have fun!" They started the music, and everything just started to feel and sound good. They served hors d'oeuvres that included shrimp, eight quarter-cut tuna sandwiches, and several different kinds of fish and salads, among other dishes. A comedian made his way to the mike and he was really funny.

Later, we danced and the music was great. We also got a beautiful surprise, BM was a wonderful blues singer! The entire group of people on the boat applauded him and urged him to sing; he did so three times. The food was amazing and we laughed a lot. It was one of the best shows I have ever seen; maybe that's not saying much, but everyone seemed to enjoy the whole spectacle. After dinner we had about thirty minutes before docking. Whether it was because we were the largest party or the youngest, I'm not sure, but the band leader asked our table what song it wanted to request, and before anybody could answer, KS said, "Sir, will you please play 'God Bless America'?" The band leader responded by saying, "It will be a pleasure." I have never heard a more beautiful rendition of that song. It was unforgettable. The band played it in a low key, and after playing it, the leader asked, "Will the crowd please sing with us?" The crowd obliged, and its rendition was the prettiest I have ever heard, perhaps because it was about sixty voices in forty different tones. After the boat docked, everyone felt a special unity after that song, and we were all saying hello to each other, another heart-warming moment that capped off a stupendous evening.

After we got off the boat, everyone in our party was in a wonderful mood, but I couldn't let the good vibe last—I had to try and find out what happened to the group that included HH, PA, WJ, and their friends. I went to the office and asked if anyone had heard anything from or about them. The clerk at the desk excused himself and went into the back office. A night manager came to the counter and said that my men and their lady friends had been detained on another part of the property. I asked, "For what?" and the night manager looked at some papers and said, "They are being charged for trespassing."

"Are they being held by officers?" I demanded.

"No, because they said that they were with a special group and we decided to hold and wait to talk with a Mr. HB. That is all the information they would give us."

"What are their fines?"

The manager replied, "$250 USD each tonight, or go to court and pay $350 USD each for court costs and the fines."

"I am, Mr. HB."

"Mr. HB, would you like to take care of this matter?"

"Where are they and what will it cost to get them?"

"No transportation charge is needed; our resort will take care of that."

"How long will it take?"

"About ten minutes."

I paid a bill and signed an agreement, and we got the group back after awhile.

The first thing I wanted to know was if the men and their friends were hungry and they said yes. We ordered food from the restaurant and I said, "We will see everyone involved with the law at my quarters."

After we met at the quarters, I told the group that they missed the show of the year, concluding by telling them to go get some rest.

These sorts of adventures were typical of this brief time in what we all considered to be a sort of paradise. I must say that it was the most wonderful time of my life, sealed by a meeting we had as a group the last night we spent there. At that gathering, we all agreed that it was a dreamlike time of pleasure, the greatest enjoyment we had ever experienced in our lives. I even wrote a poem to commemorate this special period in my service:

Everything

Each experience in life should add knowledge to every man;
> he should take advantage of every opportunity and use it
> every chance he can.

Vigorously, he should try to master all his tasks,

WHITE MAN'S TEARS CONQUER MY PAINS

and know or believe he is right if anyone should challenge or ask.
Enter into the phase of life that you feel you can command,
    and conquer as many challengers and competitors as you can.
Riches are the ecstasies of all financiers' goal,
    but respect, trust, intelligence and faith are the true making of a person with a real, real soul.
"Yesterday" is the word that truly means the past—
    the black man today wants something real that he knows will last.
Time has proven we have to insist, argue, challenge, and fight
    for everything we believe in and think is good and right.
Have we forgotten yesterday, and all its promises, heartaches, and sorrows?
    No, that's why we are insisting on knowing there will be a better tomorrow.
In time, we know society will realize and see:
    all we really want is recognition, respect, and to be completely free.
Never will we compromise for being a second-class race;
    this is something all must believe, accept, acknowledge and face.
God gave all of us the knowledge to live, prosper, know, respect and exist,
    and all these things we've been denied, and these are the things we miss.
"Everything" is a complete word for the financiers.
"Everything" is a complete word for a person who is well trained, and when it comes to life itself—

Everything is Everything.

I don't believe I ever felt more relieved than after writing this poem. I didn't know where my life would end after that tour of service for the government, but I could say that I chose the style of my life and did it my way.

My mind was filled with all kinds of thoughts in that tropical paradise. I felt like I had spilled out everything in my soul through that poem. My spirit felt bone dry when I was finished.

I reflected on my childhood heroes, the people that I had wanted to imitate in life and the image I wanted to create for myself as I interacted with my fellow man, of all colors. You think about these types of things when you are not sure if you will live much longer than your next assignment. The fact that we had lost one of our group in the last mission gave me pause as I sat there that night in Baguio. I knew that another assignment was imminent, and I hoped that I would have the wisdom and good fortune to lead my men in it with minimal—or no—losses.

The amazing treatment that we were receiving at Baguio, all on the army's tab, made me wonder just how difficult our next operation would be. How else could one justify the unlimited food that we had access to, the free lodging and entertainment, the healthy cash flow we enjoyed, making sexual intimacy possible for the men—the type of first class treatment that only high-upper class people enjoy.

I looked around at my men's excited faces, excited for so many reasons—sexual satisfaction, the happy buzz that alcohol can bring, the extreme camaraderie we all felt, even though we only used initials to refer to each other. I thought of LS, whom we lost during our first task. Oh, how I wished he could have been with us during our nearly two weeks of the high life. LS was so, so young and so, so brave. He left an indelible impression on me, even though I knew him for a very short time.

I wondered if the men who were virgins when we arrived in Baguio would ever have sex again. I wondered if the men who had a bit of experience before that raucous two weeks had enjoyed their final times in bed with a woman. I wondered most of all

WHITE MAN'S TEARS CONQUER MY PAINS

about just what the army had cooked up for us after treating a group of black men like the king of England.

CHAPTER TWELVE

Second Assignment

Barrack 15 will be assigned to Camp O'Donnell December 22, '46.

The following is information T/S HB and his group left for us in saying good-bye.

"Meeting was held, and private personnel were present to discuss an assignment unknown to news specialist. It was later learned that the meeting was to put together a plan to locate a large supply drop of medicines and food. The group was very successful in its last assignments, and is comprised of all private names and personnel. We are not aware of the number of members. The officers in the meeting were from the Sixth Bombardment Squad, Special Agents from Washington, D.C., and officers from Camp O'Donnell. Meeting lasted five hours and twenty minutes, and we don't have any idea as to destination. This is good bye from the group."

This was the official message left for a backup crew that might have been needed to capture the drop made for the U.S. forces on December 12, 1946. My men and I had no idea how easy or difficult it would be to secure these supplies. Baguio seemed a long way away, a memory that we were not sure was real or imagined.

The fifteenth group prepared to leave on assignment and completed its preparations as it gathered supplies, equipment, and instructions. We began our travel by vehicle for quite a few miles over six hours time. We came to government establishments, and the personnel there were expecting us. They gave us warm food and good instructions on the supply drop, and they let us know that there were Japanese soldiers in these areas. We didn't proceed any further in the vehicle. It was about 1800 hours. We cleaned up and took naps until 2240 hours. We left at 2300 hours, the darkness shrouding the jungle in an extra thick layer of black.

After about two-and-a-half hours of walking, we encountered Japanese soldiers, which forced us to adjust our plans over the next half hour. We trapped these soldiers and took care of the situation, then made contact with other personnel and devised more plans with them.

After another ninety minutes of walking, we smelled and saw smoke. We went into a special formation and commenced communications in code. We were about 200 yards from the covered stack, the supply drop we were meant to secure. It did not look as if it were orphaned in the jungle. About one hundred yards away from the drop, we crawled until I gave the signal to stop. After about ten seconds, I gave the signal to back out for a retreat. I could tell that the enemy was camped around the drop and we would need to alter our plan.

All of a sudden a Japanese soldier stood up and made a loud hoot with his arms stretched out. One of our soldiers fired a shot in panic, and in three to four seconds, the hill lit up like morning and the fire fight was on. The Japanese had indeed captured the drop long before we had arrived, and they would not give it up without a fierce fight.

I saw about twenty Japanese soldiers swarming on the hill. I killed a few of them, then found myself face to face with an enemy soldier. In the moonlight, we looked at each other dead straight in the eye, barely breathing as we tensed up and thought we could remain undetected somehow. This was a moment that every soldier trained for, *mano-a-mano*. I thought to myself, *That's all right, you son of a bitch, I'll get you because I know you have to move.* As I waited for him to move, something hit my right side, piercing it. I was not sure if it was a bullet or a bolo knife, the machete-like weapon that we used to clear brush in the jungle. Those razor-sharp, giant knives could cut a tree down like a little leaf; they were large, lethal weapons.

After that brief sensation of being struck in my right side, my Japanese opponent swung his bolo knife straight down on top of my head, hoping to cut it like a coconut.

Thunk!

The blade sunk into my skull, but he did not separate one side of my brain from the other, fortunately.

I fell on my back but raised my right hand in an instinctive response to fight back. His bolo found my hand.

Phwhip!

It cut one finger clean off, with three others left dangling.

I felt a heat-like sensation, then a cold sensation, then I closed my eyes as they quickly filled with the blood that was pouring from my skull. As I did that, my attacker was struck by a bullet. The impact launched him into the air and he landed right on top of me! He fell across my body as I fell onto my radio.

Then…darkness.

I passed out.

I woke up in a field hospital several days later in Manila. I had indeed been shot or cut in my right side. I was treated for that injury but was never told what had happened. Now that I am writing this memoir, I have realized after sixty-eight years of thought, that the people who had fed us near to the drop site were probably the people who saved my life.

Of the fourteen members of the fifteenth group, I was the sole survivor. Baguio was my men's swan song, one last blow-out party before the grim reaper approached so quickly. The army had at least given the men in my group a couple of weeks of pleasure before they faced insurmountable odds in a Filipino jungle. I loved every one of those men, and I am not sure how or why I alone survived. God's grace in my life was again evident. May all of my men rest in peace.

CHAPTER THIRTEEN

Field Hospital Stay

I lay there in bed trying to realize how I had survived a near-certain death, even wondering if I would escape the reaper's scythe. My life hung in the balance; I knew that. I wondered how many others had made it out of that killing field alive.

Where am I? Can I move? When will someone come and talk to me? Can I talk? Can I see? Maybe if I holler, maybe somebody will come to me. I can't talk. I can't open my mouth. I'm hurting. I'm going to smother to death. Why doesn't somebody see that I am in need of attention? Maybe I am a prisoner. Yes, that's probably what is happening.

I'm tired.

A nurse came in and tried to talk to me. She kept trying to get a response to her questions. I could not answer, but I quickly realized that I was not a prisoner of war. I was in an American hospital! I was ecstatic, although no one could tell.

The nurse left, and after awhile, a doctor came to me. It was obvious that he wanted to communicate with me too, somehow. I was not up to holding my end of the bargain on that one.

The doctor started talking to another doctor, and he seemed to be taking the bandages off my head a little at a time. He tried to talk to me, but the words in my head never made it to my lips. *Damn! Maybe my voice is gone.*

Guardian angels come in all shapes and sizes. They have unique personalities and foibles. My guardian angel, for whom I thank God to this day, was a man who loved the bottle a little too much, but who loved his patients as well. I know. He loved me and he demonstrated it with tangible actions.

Dr. May almost always smelled like a drunk, and as he looked at my wounds as the bandages came off, he was cursing angrily about my head cut. From what he said, it sounded as if that cut could have killed me eventually, if not properly cared for. I didn't think it was that bad, but he was telling the nurse adamantly to clean it twice a day. He said, "Doll, I don't give a damn. I just want this kid to live and go back home to the same shit he left." He then asked her to bring back some medicine and other items. He kept trying to talk to me, but I couldn't answer. Finally, he said quietly, "Get some rest."

The nurse came back and they worked together on my head wound. She said, "This is—." In retrospect, I think she used the word "gangrene," which would have meant curtains for me if it set in.

Dr. May replied, "I want this cleaned again in three hours, and before you leave, give it another cleaning. Have the person that replaces you to clean the cut three times."

I didn't know when they left, but I continued to be deeply joyful that I was in the care of Americans. The nurse who replaced the first nurse looked at my right hand and side. She didn't try to talk to me, but she was nice. Before she left, she said, "Good night," and she turned the light off.

I continued to rejoice in my bed, even though no one could know what was going on in my head.

Dr. May came in about two hours after the second nurse and said, "Are you ready to at least say, hello?" He took a scope and looked into my eyes and said, "How do you feel? You can talk when you get ready."

I wanted to smile. I guess I didn't because after he checked my side, my right hand, and head, he said, "You will be just fine." This treatment went on for two or three days. One morning, one nurse and two men came in and took off all the bandages and cleaned me up completely.

I was in intense pain, but at the same time I felt clean, new, after that washing. I went back to sleep before they left.

Later, a group returned, which included Dr. May, whom I saw and recognized. Despite smelling the odor of liquor all around him, I felt safe and relieved. One man asked why I was in that hospital and Dr. May pointed out that I was an American soldier, and that if the man did not see it his way, he could excuse himself from the premises.

My guardian angel saved my life and my livelihood when he refused to obey the Colonel's orders to cut my hand to the wrist, insisting that he could save at least three fingers. I will never forget Dr. May's integrity and commitment to restoring this patient to full health. Life would have unfolded very differently for me without a hand. I have Dr. May to thank for saving it.

I will never forget that Colonel's question, however. Those seven words said so much about how certain people in the military felt about blacks during that time. Some words never leave y our memory. His question will never leave mine:

"Save three fingers on a nigger's hand?"

It still hurts to even write that.

The crowd of doctors and nurses moved on through the hallways of the hospital wards. I lay there motionless. I was not angry. In fact, I smiled inwardly with joy because I realized that I had a friend in this hospital, an angel. God had sent him to protect me.

WHITE MAN'S TEARS CONQUER MY PAINS

The nurse on duty that day came in and asked me how I felt. I smiled. She said, "That is the first smile I have seen from you. Can you hear me?"

I wanted to speak, but I couldn't get my mind to cooperate with my mouth.

She continued: "My name is Mary. Blink one time if you hear me."

I blinked once.

"Very good. We would like to feed you something light, like Jell-o. Blink once for yes and two times for no."

I blinked twice.

"Thanks. That's enough for today."

The patient next to me, who I later learned was named Wilbur and hailed from Bluefield, West Virginia, said, "Ms. Mary, can I ask you a few things about this patient?"

"What would you like to know?" she said.

"Ask him if I can borrow a cigarette," and he laughed.

"I will not do that," Mary replied.

The patient said, "Can he hear?"

"Yes."

He doubled his fist and said, "I knew he could. I knew he could."

"What are you talking about?"

"I overheard an officer tell Dr. May to cut his hand off at the wrist, and Dr. May said, 'But I think I can save at least three fingers,' and the officer said, 'Save a nigger's hand?'"

I saw this patient for the first time at that moment. He smiled. It sent chills through me.

He continued: "Who is he, and why is a black man in here as a patient?"

"For the same reason as you," Mary said. "He is an American soldier fighting for his country." She got up and left. I played like I was asleep, but I heard every word.

I knew nurses were smart, but Mary showed a level of wisdom that many people did not possess in 1946. Mary consistently protected me and made statements that let people know how she felt about her prized patient, even if I was of another color. You don't forget the hurtful words people say; likewise, you don't forget the encouraging words either.

I have heard so many mean statements made to me on account of my skin tone that they do not bother me much. One thing I cannot change is the color of my skin. Such degrading statements about me as a black man didn't trouble me much back then and they don't now, but as I lay near death during that time, it was wonderful to know that I had a good doctor and caring nurses in my corner, people who saw me as a human being fighting for life, not as a black man. This is the height of adhering to the Hippocratic Oath: giving the best care possible to anyone who needs it, regardless of race, religion, or culture. The medical personnel in that field hospital lived this out every day in my case, and I am forever grateful.

On another occasion, Mary said, "Wilbur is out of cigarettes. Blink once if I can give him a pack of yours."

I blinked once.

She took the cigarettes out of my drawer and reported, "You know, he likes and respects you a lot."

I blinked once to acknowledge her compliment.

She smiled and left the cigarettes on his dresser.

Doctor May came in later and looked at my head and my side. He sat on the bed and said, "Mr. HB, how do you feel today? Do you feel like speaking to me today? I was told you can hear. Can you hear me?"

I tried with every muscle in my body and heart to speak. Dr. May put his hands on my face and said, "Please help me understand how to communicate with you. I know you can hear me. Do you know how much I want to help you?"

Smelling his breath, I realized that he had just enjoyed a nip—or more—and his red eyes confirmed my suspicion. I didn't care. My life was in his hands. Even an alcoholic can do good in this world. My angel had a weakness for the sauce. I will never hold that against him.

Dr. May said, "Do you know how much I want to hear you?"

I was finally able to say, "Yes, sir."

In a flash, he and Nurse Mary were holding my face and crying like babies. I looked over, and the patient in the next bed was crying too. Everyone sat there and no one tried to hide their feelings. It was a beautiful moment.

Dr. May finally looked around and said, "Damn! I feel good." He got up and walked back to the office.

Mary gave a fitting statement of conclusion, "I never saw this happen before."

That's very true, more true than she could ever know. The world had never seen anyone like HB before or since.

I think these two were thrilled that they had saved my life, and they were justifiably proud of their care for me. The day I was able to speak to them, they knew that I would make it, and perhaps I did too. I still had a long way to go to lead any kind of normal life, however. Surgery was in my near future.

CHAPTER FOURTEEN

Day of Surgery

First Lieutenant May announced that he would operate on me in ten hours. I was sent to surgery at 0630 and remained in surgery until 1440 hours, more than eight hours of delicate work. I then was returned to the ward.

Dr. May did not have much to say only, "I am very pleased with the results."

My head was put on what was called "special treatment," meaning that a specially trained person had to sit by my bedside 24/7 to give me care as needed after such a delicate and thorough operation. This person sat by me for several days.

I, meanwhile, was experiencing a new phenomenon that thrilled me to no end: I could again have clear conversations. Don't ever take your ability to communicate with others for granted. Once you are unable to do this for many days, you realize how central to our humanity it is to be able to talk with others, to connect with other human beings. It is part of what makes

WHITE MAN'S TEARS CONQUER MY PAINS

us human, and to have it taken away, even for a brief time, brings an incredible sadness to the soul.

After the operation, I lay in my bed for several minutes and Wilbur asked the person assigned to me if he could visit with me. The fellow assigned to me said, "Yes, for a few minutes."

Wilbur asked, "How do you feel?"

I responded, "Great."

His next words were, "Hell, man, what happened before surgery? You got everybody crying. I even shed a couple of tears. Are you a religious leader?"

I said, "Wilbur, it would take more than that to change you." We both laughed and he said, "You are talking."

"Yes." We erupted again in laughter and had a nice conversation.

Wilbur asked, "What does everybody call you?"

"By my name."

"What is that?"

"HB."

He went over and took the schedule pad off the end of the bed and asked, "What the hell does that mean?"

"That's my name."

Wilbur reached in his pajama pocket and pulled out a cigarette pack with one cigarette and said, "Oh shit, that's my last." He looked at me, half smiled and said, "Lend me a pack until I get my allowance in a couple of days."

I replied, "Not now and never."

He said, "Man, I'm not going anywhere and I'm good for it."

"The subject is closed."

He mumbled, "Man, I'm good for it."

I immediately slid down in my bed and turned my back, sending what I hoped would be an unmistakable signal.

Wilbur asked, "What will a pack cost?"

"One dollar."

"Hell, I can buy a pack for thirty to fifty cents."

"That's your best bet."

He lay there for about ten minutes smoking his last cigarette. Eventually, he came up with the dollar and shared, "I thought we were friends."

I replied, "No, bedmates."

He didn't say another word to me until a day after he and I got our allowance from the Red Cross. Nurse Mary brought us the cigarettes and said, "Nice to see that you two make such good friends."

I said, "Yes, he's the first person I've met since I've been in the service that I like talking with."

She said, "That's nice," and she turned and walked away.

Wilbur said, "Man, you have talked to the doctor four times since you said a word to me and you call me a friend."

"I didn't call you a friend. I said I like talking with you."

"You and Dr. May sure got close."

"Yes, he saved my life."

Man, you know you are going home when you leave this devil's hole, so why can't you tell me what your duty was?"

"First, I don't think this field hospital is a devil's hole. I feel I am damn lucky to be here. If I had waited, I may have met a doctor like the colonel." I looked at Wilbur and lay down.

Wilbur looked at me and said, "You are so much smarter than me. I wish we were friends. I could learn so much from you and you could help me write my dad."

"My hand is hurt. Helping to write your father doesn't come under friendship. That comes under bed mates. Maybe after dinner."

"Okay."

After Wilbur and I wrote the letter to his dad, he said, "Pops knows damn well I didn't write this letter, but he will never know a black man did."

"You are right," I said, and we hugged.

Later, Dr. May came in and said to me, "How are things today?"

I said, "Sir, I feel great, and I do have a good appetite."

He looked at the fellow sitting at my bedside and asked, "How are things going?"

He replied, "Here are my notes."

Dr. May read the notes and walked a few steps with the assigned person. They talked for a few minutes and Dr. May said, "Thanks, and keep up the good work." He then returned and checked my head, side, and hand. He finally said, "Drink more water."

I replied, "Yes, sir." He smiled and walked away, happy that I had made it and that he had again used his gifts and training to save a man's life.

CHAPTER FIFTEEN

Beginning of Recovery

Later, I was reassigned to Dr. Stanley McCabe, from Utah, and he gave me a preview of things to come by spending the first half of the day caring for me by trying to find out why I was with a Detachment 1 unit. Finally, he was told that I was with a special unit and I was to be treated as a top priority. That did not seem to give him the proper respect for me, and my recovery would be spiced with no shortage of drama.

The first time we talked, he asked me insistently what my first name was.

I replied, as I always did, "HB, sir."

His answer? "Don't give me that shit!"

I calmly said, "Yes, sir," and he asked again, "What is your name?"

I looked at him and said, "If you think you will have a problem working with me, sir, then I suggest you get me assigned to someone else."

WHITE MAN'S TEARS CONQUER MY PAINS

He answered, "I'm not used to working on niggers."

I said, a little less patiently, "You had better turn me over to someone else. I need a doctor, not a problem. Hell, we are fighting the same war, and I don't trust your kind." I refused to speak any further with him.

Dr. May came in at about 1500 hours, looked at me and Dr. McCabe, and asked, "What is the problem?"

After a moment of silence, Dr. McCabe said, "This boy don't seem to want to cooperate."

Dr. May looked at Dr. McCabe, then peered at me and asked, "Sgt. HB, what seems to be the problem?"

I serenely said, "Sir, this doctor doesn't want to work with this nigger boy and I don't want him on this job. Dr. May, sir, you saved my life, and it's too precious to trust him with me.

Dr. May asked, "Stanley, what happened? Did you use the 'n word'?" He dropped his head and admitted, "I guess I did get a little rough with him, but I thought he was tougher than that. I apologize if I offended him."

Dr. May looked at me and asked, "Well, HB?"

I stood there for about three or four seconds, thinking of what to say. It was again time to speak up for myself and guard the dignity that I had. I announced, "I didn't come this far, and I never will accept a person of his character to call me the 'n word,' and I refuse his service with me, sir."

"Well, Sgt. HB," Dr. May said, "What would you like to do?"

I sneered, "I'm a soldier; I like to kill."

Dr. McCabe got the message and quickly said, "I'll find a replacement for me." He looked at Dr. May and me and walked away.

Dr. May was in disbelief about the whole scene. He asked, "Are you kidding?"

I said, "No, sir."

He should have known better, but I guess we hadn't spent enough time talking because I was at death's door for so long and could not interact with him. He was getting to know me now.

Dr. May came back about 2015 hours and looked at my side, the fingers on my right hand, and my head. He said, "The fingers and side are looking fine and the head is amazing."

I said, "Sir, they all feel fine. Thanks again for giving me my life. Can you imagine Dr. McCabe giving me the surgery you performed?"

Dr. May said, "I came by to show you something." He raised his collar and showed me his captain bars. I was thrilled for him.

He said quietly, "I didn't know I could stay sober long enough to accept them."

I said, "Sir, I don't think being sober got them for you. I am sure being a great doctor had a lot to do with it. Dr. May, before I could see you I smelled the liquor, and I was so glad to smell the liquor. I knew you were there and I felt safe. Dr. May, your tears conquered my pains. That is why I had a very easy recovery. God gave you the talent and strength to give me back my life, and I shall cherish you forever for the trust He had in you."

Captain May stood there with tears in his eyes again, and said, "I gave you nothing compared to what you gave me." He came over to my bed, put my left hand into his hands, and just held it there. He eventually dropped my hand and walked away, overcome with emotion.

Dr. McCabe later promised to never treat me again alone as long as I was in that ward, and I agreed. He turned out to be as nice as a person could be, someone who tried to correct inborn bad habits. I learned to truly respect him in time, and he did the same for me.

This was a constant theme during my military service, as you can discern from these pages. As I interacted with white soldiers of all different ranks, we usually came to a point of mutual respect. I would like to think that I changed dozens of men's attitudes about blacks during my brief time in the military. I am sure my efforts were multiplied many times by black soldiers throughout all branches of the Armed Forces. Perhaps we planted the seeds that would lead to the Civil Rights movement and the place that we now hold in American society.

World War II brought blacks and whites into close quarters together, and we discovered that we were all human beings, created in God's image and worthy of complete respect because of that alone, no matter what type of pigmentation we had. Dr. McCabe was just another example of someone overcoming his past to see blacks in a new way. I was happy to give him that new perspective, but I had to initiate that process by standing my ground and protecting my self-respect.

CHAPTER SIXTEEN

Rehabilitation Period

After such an intense surgery, and with the severe injury to my hand, I of course needed rehabilitation. A very nice group of people was assigned to me, to help me heal enough to go back to civilian life in the U.S. A few days later, a meeting about my lodging arrangements was held. It was a bit complicated because the government did not have regular living quarters for me and I didn't need any if I was being honorably discharged. Because of that status, I was eligible to get clearance from the Quartermaster and the hospital. I spoke with Captain May and he said he looked forward to examining me for discharge from the hospital.

At the meeting regarding my post-discharge housing, representatives from the Quartermaster, including various lieutenant colonels, Nurse Mary, Captain May and the moderator for the meeting, Lt. McCabe. I was the first person called.

Lt. McCabe asked, "T/S HB, is there a simpler name I can call you except T/S HB?"

WHITE MAN'S TEARS CONQUER MY PAINS

"Yes, sir, you may call me Sgt. HB."

"Sgt. HB, do you know why you are here?"

"Yes, sir."

"How do you intend to handle this situation?"

"Lt. McCabe, I am not here to tell the U.S. what to do with me. I am here to listen and hope we can understand each other and get this situation straightened out, since it is not a law-breaking situation."

A lieutenant colonel raised his hand and asked, "May I interrupt."

Lt. McCabe responded, "Yes, sir."

The officer said, "This is not a court-type situation. We can handle this in a more common manner. I realize we are dealing with a special-type soldier. I suggest we make this a private meeting and we will settle in a personal and respectful manner."

Everyone agreed with this suggestion, so the group got together and devised a solution in about fifteen minutes. The conclusion was that I would have a simple release from duty and my papers processed as a normal American soldier.

Lt. Colonel Schults, the officer who had suggested the private meeting, said to me, "Sgt. HB, may I have a private meeting with you?"

I replied, "It would be a pleasure, sir."

We walked over to the administration area into an office. He offered me a drink. I accepted a soda. We shook hands and he said, "Sgt. HB...," and he sat and just looked at me for a moment. "How do I say I'm damn proud of you and the group? I know of two and maybe three plane jobs you were a part of. You are just a baby. You saved many lives and maybe your own when you did that last drop. The jet plane job had a $10 million price tag on the documents if returned, and a black soldier about your age was found at the scene and they wanted to call him a terrorist or plane robber. Do you know anything about that wreck?"

"Sir," I started, "I am not in a position to discuss anything concerning assignments. We couldn't do anything about that anyway, but I thank you."

He continued, "I do know about the Baguio Resort reservation and the results, the behavior was superb. Sgt. HB, what I am really saying is your group Barrack 15 has left a great heroic trail and I'm not asking anything else. If you have any problems, take this and get in touch with me," he said as he handed me his card. "I wish I could do more to help or reward you. Thank you for your service."

Of course, I felt ten feet tall after that meeting.

It had been a long and emotional day and I went back to the ward to get some sleep. Wilbur had other ideas. He said, "Ain't you going to talk to me? I have been waiting for you like you were my old lady." He laughed at his own humor.

I said, "Wilbur, I have to rest. Man, I am so tired I can't keep my eyes open."

"Mary gave me a pack of your cigarettes."

"I know. I told her to."

"Thanks."

I turned over and went to sleep. I slept a few hours and felt much better.

Later, Wilbur said, "Man, tell me what happened. Are you being shipped out or going to jail?"

"Why would I be going to jail? Everybody I killed was legal."

"HB, you are not in this ward by mistake. You are here because you are a bad fucker. FBI, CIA, or private investigator?"

"No, nothing like that."

"But HB, there were people here talking about you like they are afraid to mess with you."

"Like who?"

"Well, I can't just come out like I'm gossiping."

"Well, you are."

"Are they going to make you move out?"

I asked, "Why would they?"

"Why would you want to stay in here with us dumb whiteys?"

"Because we are all American soldiers."

"Bullshit, HB. Some of us are fuckin' dummies but not you. HB, we saw you walking across the lawn and going to one of those offices with an officer they call God. No shit. Who are you?"

"Wilbur, cool down, man. That was personal business. I'm trying to convince these people that I'm on America's side." I smiled.

We then sat around and joked and talked about nothing too important. Wilbur later said, "HB, why did you give Nurse Mary authority to give me your cigarettes?"

"Because she and I decided you would kill if you didn't get your cigarettes."

Someone came by and asked me if I wanted them to bring me dinner. I said yes.

Wilbur piped up, "What about me?"

I said, "This service is for blacks only," and I laughed.

The next morning, Wilbur had to go for his exam, and he found out he would be going home in a few days. We were told by a nurse that the hospital was having a patients' boat tour in a couple of days and that we had to sign up for it by requesting a spot through the nurse on our ward. Wilbur and I decided to see if we could get permits to go. When Mary came around we asked and then signed up for the tour. That was the first time I had been on any entertainment function since being in service. We all gathered on three buses and went about three miles to a beautiful lake. There were about 150 patients. The sponsors had all kinds of food, soda, beer, nurses, nurses' aides and two or three doctors, along with a disc jockey. It was a lot of fun. We sang, danced, played games, and had a comedian that told jokes.

Wilbur and I lay at the front of the boat where the water sprayed on the boat, and we both went to sleep. Wilbur woke up screaming. He had a bright red back with a swath of sunburn about eight to ten inches wide and twelve to fourteen inches long that turned into blisters almost a half inch high an hour later. He was picked up by a speedboat and rushed back to the hospital. I saw him a few days later in another ward. We exchanged a lot of jokes about that fact that I didn't have any blisters on my back; it was just shiny and black. We made a lot of racial comments that we would not have made to other people. It was so refreshing to make racial statements and realize that such comments could be made without offending the other person *if* the relationship was strong.

After about five weeks Wilbur received his papers for departure to Hawaii. That was a great day. The following weekend we got passes and went to Manila and had a nice time. We were going to get two chicks and spend the evening or night with them, but I got cold feet and he also backed out. We used the excuse of, "What if we got a disease and took it back home?"

We spent the night at a hotel and had a nice breakfast. We talked about what he and I were going to do about Hawaii. Since Wilbur was leaving before me, he decided to send me a message about where he was going for his discharge. I had told him that I was going to try and get my discharge in Detroit, Michigan, because my sister lived in Detroit and that would give me a chance to visit with her and the government would pay for my trip to Texas because that was home for me. He said he had a brother in North Carolina and might get his discharge in North Carolina for the same reason I was getting mine in Detroit.

In Manila, we visited beautiful gardens, other special sites and went to downtown to do window shopping. We finally caught a cab and went back to the hospital in the evening. One day we were just talking and he said, "Man, what the hell did you come in the service for? When you get out you are going to live in the same crap and sit behind me the same as you did before you went in the service."

I replied, "You are damn right. I am going to sit in the back if I come and ride the bus or streetcar, but I intend to buy a car and splash water on your ass if you are still waiting for a bus or streetcar!"

And that's how I had to look at it all as my time in the service drew to a close. Even someone who was not particularly brilliant such as Wilbur understood that I would be returning to a country where I would again have to sit in the back of the bus, even though I had nearly given my life in service to that country. I did not plan on riding a bus though, as I said to Wilbur. I was going to use my service as a springboard to a better life, to driving my own automobile, in which I could sit anywhere I wanted.

CHAPTER SEVENTEEN

So Long To a Friend

The day before Wilbur left, we sat on a bench under a tree on the lawn at the field hospital and reminisced about everything from my first day at the hospital until the day he had learned he was leaving for a discharge in the United States. It was very interesting and educational to hear his perspective. I think it gave me a deeper appreciation for being alive and all that my doctors had done for me.

Wilbur said that when I was brought into the hospital, there were about five people with me, and to him I looked like a mummy. "The hospital people with the bed you were wheeled in with left, but two doctors and a nurse remained with you. Everybody was talking a lot of medical talk. When one doctor left, another doctor came in and the nurse left, and Dr. May came in and looked at your schedule and they stayed there and talked. Finally, two technicians came in with a curtain that they put around a patient's bed when they want to operate in the ward.

They covered everything, and about five people were behind the curtains working on you. About two hours passed and people came in and people left. It came time for me to go for lunch, but for some reason I just couldn't leave my bed so I just missed lunch. Two technicians came to the curtains and they let them in with a medicine rack. They hung several lines on your body; there seemed to be about six different lines running in your body. I finally heard Dr. May say, 'You're damn right he will live!' and he and two or three had discussions. Finally, things got quiet behind the curtain and they worked on you for about three and a half hours. The crowd began to thin out one at a time. Dr May left for about thirty or forty minutes, and others left until a group came in and took out some things, including the medicine racks and curtains. I looked close and all I could see was holes so you could breathe and hear, and a small cut to answer through, but not wide enough to talk."

"They had a bandage on your head that was the strangest I ever saw. Nurse Mary stayed there and I knew she would tell me something, so I looked her straight in the eyes and said, 'What happened to this soldier?' and 'Will he live?' She said, 'We won't know for a few days.' I said, 'Why did they work on him in the ward instead of the operation room?' She looked around and said, 'He couldn't wait for an open bed.'"

"The Red Cross came by with stuff that they usually leave for patients. The Red Cross representative looked at Mary and started giving you the regular package that they leave for patients. She asked, 'Does he smoke?' Mary said, 'Just give him the full package, including cigarettes.' Mary usually smiles and talks to us and the Red Cross, but for some reason she didn't have much to say about anything. Mary said to me, 'I had them save your lunch. You'd better go before the mess hall starts dinner.' Hell, man, she was like a mother in so many ways!"

"I don't know who or what I thought you was, but I never thought you were a black soldier. I figured you may be a captured Japanese officer, private agent like CIA, FBI, or somebody special like that because there were so many concerned people there to see you. Some didn't come to your bed; they would just come to the corner of your side of the ward and stand and talk for a few minutes and leave. I found out you were a black soldier when they came in and put the curtain around your bed and spent a lot of time cleaning you up for this special showing, for the doctors that decide what operation you get. When they looked at you, this colonel told Dr. May to cut your hand off at the wrist and Dr. May said, 'But, sir, I can save at least three fingers.' The colonel turned around, looked at you and said to Dr. May, 'Save three fingers on a nigger's hand?' Dr. May looked like he wanted to cry. That was when I realized you were black and something hit me in the inside of my stomach and I wanted to just get up and curse that colonel out. Man, I lay there pissed off and I don't know, but I felt sorry for you and I knew a time that I would have said, 'Right on.' From that day on I wanted to see you, talk to you. I was jealous of the feeling you and the doctor had for each other."

Wilbur said he really didn't know how nice it was to want to be with someone as a friend until he met me. He said the day I was admitted to that hospital, his life changed, just looking at a mummy-style body of a person without even knowing the person's race. "I feel like my whole life is being left at this field hospital in another country," he said.

I replied, "Wilbur, my life has never been automatic. I wake up every day hoping to be able to experience something different that enables me to make the statement, if just to myself, at the end of the day that says, 'Damn, sure was a good day.' Like the day I spoke my first word to Dr. May and he said, 'Damn, I feel good.'"

"I've had that feeling about twice in my life," Wilbur observed. "That is a good feeling."

"That first day in the field hospital in the Philippine Islands was the beginning of a wonderful experience in my life, as I lay back and let a group of strangers save the only life that God gave me," I continued. "I was placed in the hospital next to a very young and curious Southern white man who was as naïve as the young black man in the bed next to him, both there offering their lives to fight for their country. I was very happy to meet an American; it's like being in a country on vacation and you really don't know anybody. It becomes lonely so quick, but as soon as I looked at you, Wilbur, I knew you and I would become friends because I do know how to make friends. When you jumped up and down in bed and said, 'I knew it! I knew it! I knew he could hear it when that colonel said, "Save a nigger's three fingers?" Mary, that damn doctor said that to Dr. May and it pissed me off.' That's when I knew I had a friend-to-be in this ward.

"Wilbur, I want you to know you have been as important to my survival as anything or anybody. Each feeling has its own strength of human value." I stood up, reached and shook his hand and said, "Take care of your dad. All these army habits and experiences you have been in could confuse a man that sent a son to war that became a man."

CHAPTER EIGHTEEN

My Final Days at the Hospital

After Wilbur left the hospital and went back to the United States for a discharge, it seemed as if that's when things started to change during my remaining days at the hospital. Dr. McCabe got to the place where he had to find some way to harass me. He would come in smiling to make anybody that noticed think that he was saying nice things to me. He would then say, "How is my hard, black-ass nigger doing?" and follow that with, "Isn't that what HB means?"

I would say, "To you, yes." I would never let him give me any medicine of any kind. Dr. McCabe made up a report and tried to have me transferred to a black field hospital somewhere in Mindoro City. I did a little research when I heard about this. The head of the Manila Philippines Medical Center, Dr. Schults, had told me that if I ever needed him to call him, so I did. I asked if he knew anything about the black field hospital. He said, "Yes, it's a hellhole." Dr Schults got in touch with Dr. McCabe and he came to me and apologized.

About three or four days later Dr. McCabe was transferred to a hospital in Mindanao, Davao. Mary the nurse told me to keep it to myself and that Captain May had something to do with it. Captain May had a news release about the medicine the hospital had received in the last month, and he said it was a group of brave Americans that had caused that shipment to be possible. He also said that he wasn't positive, but the personnel at the Field Hospital of East Manila may have had at least one brave soldier from the group as a patient. He went on to name some of the properties that were recaptured.

I lay there in bed and thought about how Wilbur had sat up in bed with his fist doubled and said, "I knew it, I knew it. I knew he could hear." God, how I missed Wilbur. A few days after Dr. McCabe was transferred, I received my papers for transfer to Hawaii, and from there to the USA. Nurse Mary came by and said how proud she was to have met me and what a nice person I was. She added that I had helped Wilbur to be a better person. I said, "Hold it right there. Wilbur was my savior. He once told me, 'I miss you like you are my old lady.'"

Even so, my discharge was great news and everything was just fine. I had to fill out some paperwork, and it was a little strange to start answering to the name Henry Badgett. Another doctor gave me my final examination. I glanced at my record and said, "I don't see any reference concerning my head damage." The doctor said that was on my final report, which also explained treatments. I said that was fine, not knowing that the injury to my head would never be fully acknowledged by the military.

All of my belongings were handled by someone and put on a small bus. I went to the air base and waited a short while. I had a nice flight to Hawaii, and then had transportation to a hospital. I was there about three days when I was called to the front desk. A person said, "I have a telegram for you." It was from Wilbur, telling me to ask for the Percy Jones Hospital in Battle Creek,

Michigan. It was exciting to hear from him and to think that I would see him again.

When my paper work was finished, I was on my way to the U.S. By then, I was getting *really* excited. The flight was nice and I slept a lot, happy to eventually arrive in Michigan. Government transportation took me to Percy Jones Army Hospital, where I was surprised to see Wilbur waiting for me. He helped me with my belongings and showed me to the registration area, where I signed in. They gave me the same living quarters as Wilbur and we couldn't wait to start talking. The first thing he said about Percy Jones was, "Man, this place is so big I get lost every time I leave the damn room. It's like being in a big school with no classrooms, just sick rooms and waiting rooms."

I said, "Wilbur, you know you never been in a school bigger than one with a classroom, principal's office and restroom." He laughed an excited laugh and arrived at our room and set my belongings down. We shook hands and reminisced awhile about positive things. It was Friday, and I said, "What have you done exciting while you were here?" He replied, "Nothing. I was waiting for you, and guess what?

"What?"

"We can sit on the bus together!"

"No. If I had known that, hell, I would not have gone into the army. I would have just come to Michigan!"

We both had money that we had been issued in Hawaii, and $200 more as soon as we got to registration. I said, "Let's go out tonight and paint this town red."

Wilbur said, "What the hell will we wear?"

"Our uniforms, so we can dress like twin brothers." I could see the look on his face and tell how excited and naïve he was. After dinner we decided to go to a USO club recommended on an information sheet that had been posted on the bulletin board at the hospital. We caught a cab in front of the hospital and I asked the driver about the club. He said it was kind of rough and told us to just be careful. We thanked him for the ride and the advice.

WHITE MAN'S TEARS CONQUER MY PAINS

We went in and the crowd was mostly black people. We looked at each other and Wilbur said, "HB, this is new to me." I said, "How did you know I was coming today on the bus?"

"Because when I said HB, they asked what HB meant. I couldn't tell them and they looked and said, 'I think this is it.' I said the name is Henry Badgett," Wilbur said.

He continued, "Why did they call you HB?"

"That's what they called me. Now, do you want a drink?"

"Sure." We went to the bar and ordered a drink. A fellow came up and asked, "Are you guys just back from overseas?" I said, "Yes" and he said, "Then I have to get that first drink for you," and he did. He added, "Thanks for serving and welcome home." We clicked glasses and said thanks. Wilbur had a double shot of bourbon and coke and I had a coke. We went over and sat at a little table for two. I told Wilbur that most people had on civilian clothes and that made it pretty easy to know the new soldiers. The little hustler girls were easy to recognize because of the way they dressed; in contrast, girls looking for a boyfriend dressed nicely and in a respectful way.

Wilbur looked at me and said, "What do you have planned for me?" I said, "Nothing. Natural life will take care of everything. Wilbur, have you noticed the fellow that bought us the drink? He has been watching us ever since we sat down. He'll be over any time now and that girl that came by and spoke, she'll be over too. It's a matter of time; both are interested in us. Well, the girl will probably be the first because she was coming and looking at me to dance."

I eventually said yes to the girl and we started dancing. She found out that I could dance and the man found out that I wanted to party. When I got back to the table, the lady said, "You are a nice dancer," and I said, "Thanks, and so are you." She asked, "May I join you?"

I said, "Well, we just got back from overseas and we need a few more private minutes we would like to share, but if you are available a little later it will be a pleasure."

She said, "Yes, I understand," and she left. Before Wilbur could say, "Man, why didn't you let the chick sit down? I could have stood the company," the fellow was standing at the table saying, "Man, I guess you guys are ready to party."

"What's your name?" he continued.

"Just call me, HB."

Wilbur said, "Will."

The man said, "HB, man, you can cut a rug!"

"Thanks."

He said, "Looks like you guys are ready for another drink."

"Well, man, that drink sure got me ready."

He said, "Don't spend all your money at that bar. Shucks, it will break you." He opened his jacket and said, "The next drink is on me."

I said, "That sounds good to me."

He replied, "See you in a minute," and he walked off.

I said, "I didn't expect this to happen so soon."

"What do you mean?" Wilbur said.

"The man is a cheap con," I said. "He wants to get us drunk. He thinks I'm easier because I pulled my money out when he was talking. That is called flashing, and when I made that stupid move, that shows I'm weaker. Do you want to have some fun?"

Wilbur said, "What do you mean?"

"Do you want to con the con?"

"Yes, Henry, I'm into anything you want to do except kill."

I said, "Why not? That should be the only thing we know."

Wilbur said, "Are you kidding?"

"I'm not into killing anybody, but it may mean something close."

Wilbur looked at me for awhile and said, "Hell, I'm for whatever."

"I am going to act dumb and I am going to pretend that I think you want to take my money. I may give him some of my money to keep for me, but we have to get him drunk with his own liquor. You have to pretend you are getting drunk from his bottle, but you can't drink anymore. Whatever I do or say about you is a part of the game. We will let him run the game. His intention is to get me drunk because he knows I have money. Okay?"

Wilbur said, "Okay."

Sure enough, the con man came back to the table and said, "Let's go to the toilet." We followed him to the toilet. After he got into the toilet, two guys came in that called his name and said, "How about a little swig?"

The con man said, "Sure, pal," and the fellows went into the stall together. When they came out, each gave him a piece of money, about a dollar each. When they left, the con man handed the bottle to me and said, "Go take yourself a little swig."

I went in and pretended to get a drink. When I came out I gave the bottle to Wilbur. He went in and went through the same act. When Wilbur came out, he surprised me. He looked at me and said, "Pal, take care of that for us."

I said, "I guess so," and we came out of the toilet. The fellow said, "When I come back, I want to take you guys out and show you the prettiest car in town." We said, "Okay," and we went back to our table, which was now taken by other people. We stood against the wall. Wilbur said, "You are the coolest person I ever met in my life. What is our next move?"

I said, "Next, he will take us to his car and we will drink and see how much he drinks." The con man came back and the lady I danced with was talking to me about a party at her home the next night. I asked her to write down her address and phone number and give it to me. She gave me the information and walked away. The fellow returned and said, "We ready to get another little swig?"

I said, "Sure, man, I could use a drink." We went to the car and I sat in the back where I could pour the liquor on the floor. When we got in the car I said, "Man, I need pop with my drink."

The con man said, "Got it." He looked in his trunk and came out with a Coca-Cola. That was great; every time I got a swig I had a drink of pop. I started to bitch, saying, "Hey, man, you aren't drinking nothing!" He said, "Hell, man, I can out-drink you anytime."

I pulled out my money and said, "How much you want to bet?" He pulled his roll out, and I said, "Those are all dollar bills." He separated bills, and I estimated he had maybe $800 or $900.

I said, "Hell, got more than that at the hospital!"

He said, "How much you got now?"

"Maybe three or four hundred." I thought he was just playing a part. We knew then how much he had, and if he was a big enough fool to show a stranger his money, he was over the edge.

Wilbur was just watching. Eventually, I asked, "Where is the bottle?" Wilbur said, "Big money got the bottle." We took a drink together.

"Now it's time to check out who is drunk," I said. "This is the last of this bottle. Anybody want that last drink? Let's go to the liquor store."

The con man said, "I have a bottle in the car, but I'm not giving any more away."

"How much you want for the bottle?"

"Cheap ass, I want twenty dollars for the bottle."

"Where is the bottle?"

He attempted to get out of the car and stumbled. I said, "Let me help you." I got out and opened the trunk, and that was the last bottle he had. I got the bottle out and said, "Let's get back in and have a drink and relax for a while."

He got back in and the radio was low. The music was a nice blues tune. We were quiet for about three or four minutes, and then he passed out.

I said to Wilbur, "How about going to Canada?"

Wilbur looked at me and said, "Are you shitting me?"

"I never shit a friend."

We took his money, caught a cab, went to the bus station, and went to Detroit. From there, we boarded a bus and went to Windsor, Canada, where we caught a cab and went to a hotel. In Windsor, I asked the cab driver if he knew of any girls that might

WHITE MAN'S TEARS CONQUER MY PAINS

like to party with us. He told me to just ask the clerk at the hotel and they would take care of everything.

When we got to the hotel, I asked the clerk about available girls and she said, "Yes, we can take care of that for you fellows." I started asking questions, such as, "How much for the girls?" The clerk responded with her own question, "For how long?" She continued, "For an hour, it's $40 USD for the girl and $15 USD for the hotel. If you want girls for all day, that would be $150 each for the girls and $45 USD each for the hotel. I asked, "Is that like until we leave tomorrow?" The clerk said, "Yes."

I asked about food, and she said that depended on what we ate. When I asked about champagne, she said that depended on what label. I asked for a typical charge for champagne and she specified $15–$20 a bottle. I followed up by asking how much it would be for two rooms. She said, "Suppose from 3:00 today until 11:00 tomorrow, but I will let you in now even though it was only 10:15 a.m." I said, "Okay, how much for a suite?" She replied, "Sixty dollars plus tax for a suite."

I said, "We will pay you now and come back for the other things," referring to the girls. She said okay and it cost us about $100 USD for the hotel. We went up and counted the money we had. I came back down and paid for a black lady, a redhead, and a blonde. I got one quart of Jack Daniels whiskey, one large bottle of champagne, six bottles of Coca-Cola, and a menu. The clerk said the girls would be in about 4:00 p.m. Wilbur and I went downtown shopping. We bought pajamas, toothpaste, combs, brushes, and other men's things. We ate and tried to get ready for the three ladies, returning to the hotel, feeling wonderful. We had lots of money, and we were in our own world!

We dressed in our pajamas after we had bathed. The suite had one king-size bed and a reclining couch in the front room along with a refrigerator. At about 4:15, a call came from downstairs. A clerk said, "There are guests here for you." I said, "Send them up please," and they came up. They were young and beautiful.

They came in and the black lady came over and said, "Hello, hero," and I said, "Hi," and she went straight to Wilbur and asked, "May I be your plaything today?" He said, "You damn right. You can even have my heart." She said, "I suddenly hope so," and the fun began.

The redhead said, "I have been waiting to wear these pajamas for three weeks. A friend bought them for my birthday." The blonde went into the bathroom and came out in a black short pajama panty with a see-through bra, where the breast sat inside a strap. I was so excited until I thought of taking a drink, but I was afraid of how it would make me react.

I went to the fridge and asked the blonde if she wanted to open the bottle. She said, "I really don't need it," and the redhead was standing in a cream-colored one-piece with her little tits holding the sides of the suit together with the nipples just hanging. She said, "I don't need that" and took me by the hand. She and the blonde took me to the king-size bed where Wilbur had left enough room for both of us. What a start to a very memorable day! It was an indescribable experience.

As the evening went on, we all showered together and everyone had a cocktail. The girls had a whiskey and coke and so did Wilbur; I had a coke and ice. We lay six in a row in bed, some with their legs crossed, some with one leg on another person and some with their legs up and a hand on a knee or leg; all of it was fine with me. I asked the redhead what is one of her most disgusting experiences with a sex partner was, and she looked at me and said, "Do you really want to talk about something like that?"

I replied, "Not if it's a subject you don't like."

The blonde said, "I think that is a wonderful subject. I'll go first on that question. I think it is funny."

She continued, "I had a date with this really handsome American man. I couldn't wait to let him get in my pants. We met at a party after an American star had performed. I had a special invite to the party. We danced, flirted, kissed, and rubbed close on slow dances. I could feel his thing up against me. My pants were wet. Before he could ask me to his hotel, I said, "Yes, yes." I was ready.

"We got to his hotel, and I asked him if I could take a shower. I wanted no excuse not to enjoy this. When I came out of the shower, he had turned on some nice music and I was on fire. He went into the bathroom and kind of cleaned up, which was okay with me. He came in with his shorts on and I wondered why he wouldn't take his shorts off. We started messing around and I kind of tried to take his shorts off, and I couldn't understand why he wouldn't let me. I tried to put my hands on his penis, and again he fought me.

"I said, 'Okay, I'll do it his way.' He put his penis in and kept his hand on his penis. I was so ready until I just got mine, and he said, 'Wait, wait,' and he came close but didn't get his. He turned over and finished by jacking off. He told me I was too quick, and I said, 'Why didn't you take your shorts off?' He said he had a birthmark on his butt and he was ashamed of it. I was so disappointed, but I got mine."

The redhead, encouraged by this funny story, began her own tale, "I do remember an occasion I had a date with a football player and I went to a hotel with him. He was from Canada and I really did like him, but I was afraid of him—he had so many women. I was seventeen or eighteen, and I made up my mind to go with him anyway. He and I took a bath together, and I was really ready for him. We smoked a little pot and we both took a shower, but he wouldn't take a shower with me. We got in bed and he wanted to give me some head. I said, 'Okay, baby, I like that sometimes,' but he was terrible at that, so he wanted to screw me in the butt. His thing was so small he couldn't put it in. He kept trying and he could never get his thing hard enough. I got so tired of him trying until he said, 'Honey, it just didn't work,' and he gave me a $50 bill and said, 'You may not be a business lady, but you need something for your time.' We've been friends for four or five years, and I have never mentioned our incident."

The black lady was the third woman to answer my question. She said, "I do remember a time I was with a date and we had been seeing each other on several different occasions. We went to a party and had fun, and I needed some attention. He had been there when I had wanted a friend, so I made up my mind that I wanted to hit the sack with him. After the party I invited him to my place. We stopped and got some food and took it to my place. We had a few laughs and took a shower together, and I said, 'Small! What the hell? Maybe he is a good lover.' We got in bed and he started. He was rough. He used his fingers like they were an old wrench, pushing his fingers in me very hard, and he could never get his penis ready. He wanted me to do crazy things. I just refused, and I finally said, 'I can't handle this dude,' and got up."

"He sat back and cried and said, 'Can you please forgive me?' I said, 'Sure.' He then left. I got hurt from that for quite awhile."

The redhead said, "HB, I know you have a couple to share!" I sat and tried to think of something that I thought was interesting enough and finally said, "I really can't remember anything really funny, but I had an old friend that came back to town from a long trip who had a lady with a friend, and they asked me if I wanted to go on a double date with them. I said, 'Okay.' We went out to dinner and to a club, had a nice but not a super time. After we left the club we followed him and his date, and they went straight to a small hotel. He got out and I followed the couple to their room. I looked at her and she followed me into the room. I closed the door and she looked and said, 'I didn't expect this.' She sat there for about three or four minutes and said, 'Excuse me for a few minutes.' She went into the toilet and came out naked! She half-smiled and said, 'Well, I put myself in this situation. I won't disappoint you, but I won't move.' She got in bed on top of the cover and I said, 'I am sorry, but this is not my style. I am a guest, remember? Please get up. You embarrass me.'"

The party laughed and some made small comments such as, "You would do that!" "That's like you," and so on. When it was Wilbur's turn, I held my breath. He dropped his head and said,

'Well, I really don't have a hell of a lot of experience in this field, but a little chick and me was messing around one day and we decided to make a little love. She wouldn't take her pants off, so I just decided to open up the side and get a little. Man, I opened up the side, stuck it in from the side, and the panties was tight. My fingers came out of the panties and the side of the panties cut the hell out of my thing! I never tried that again!"

I think that was the winning story. We had a lovely evening and a wonderful night. I got up the next morning, cleaned up, gave the ladies an extra fifty dollars each, hugged and kissed them all, and we said beautiful good-byes to each other. Wilbur and I caught a cab, then a bus, and went back to the hospital in. It was a trip and experience that I will never forget. Wilbur and I lived like kings that weekend in Canada.

We came back from Canada that Sunday night, reported to the hospital for assignment, and for five or six days just had a wonderful time. I had met a true friend in Wilbur, and I will always remember him. We communicated for about ten or eleven years after our separation, until his father passed away from cancer. When we talked on the phone, he always said, "I love you, man."

CHAPTER NINETEEN

Concluding Thoughts

I was discharged from the service on August 29, 1947, and went back to Dallas, Texas, on September 23, 1947, to straighten out my family life. I was down one finger on my right hand from the last time I was home. It had been amputated at the metacarpal phalangeal joint. I did have three fingers with limited motion, thanks to dear Dr. May, as well as a looming arthritis condition below my right elbow, due to the new limitations of my hand.

My wife Ruby and I had both changed a lot in the intervening seventeen months, and we decided to get to know more about each other. In short, we had both become adults. I had grown up on a long boat ride, adventures in the jungle and a hospital stay that brought my life back from the brink. She, meanwhile, had raised a child on her own.

She was still as beautiful as I remembered. I learned quickly that I was not her first choice for the type of man that she wanted to settle down with. She was not looking for a soldier but a businessman with money. She also didn't believe that we shared the same values as people and she was right. I didn't say much in reply to her viewpoint, but I agreed inwardly with all that she said. I did eventually tell her that we should let bygones be bygones, yet remain friends for the sake of our son, George Edward.

We remained married but did not live together for two-and-a-half years, eventually divorcing in 1948. We parted amicably, with complete respect for each other. I moved to Denver, Colorado, and attended college, finishing a degree in Business Administration. I eventually discovered that I needed to type a lot to succeed in that field, but with my disabled right hand, that would not be possible.

The Department of Veterans Affairs regional office in Dallas recommended me to go to the Department of Veterans Affairs at Fort Logan, Colorado, to register for my physical examination to receive my disability rating from the Army. I reported to Fort Logan in 1948, and the Veterans Administration there had moved to a newly built hospital in Denver.

I made an appointment and visited the hospital three days straight, but was refused service. I got in touch with the VA and it sent me a letter that I had to take to the Veterans Hospital within ninety days for my final examination to get an evaluation for my disability rating. The VA did not include my head injury because it did not show on my records as occurring in service, so I was disallowed any consideration in my rating due to the injury to my head. That was a color thing and I refused to fight it. You need two things to fight injustice, money and pride; and attorneys don't accept pride.

Despite slights like this, I have been too blessed in my life to complain about such shortcomings in our society. I have held onto God's gift of eighty-six years of truly precious living. The last thirty-nine years have been with the most wonderful lady in this world. She is a priceless gift.

I later built a career in building maintenance and stayed in that field until my retirement.

Ruby married a wonderful man and went on to have a lovely family.

As for George Edward, he went into the service like his daddy. And, like his father, he was disabled as a result of his time in the Armed Forces. He married a wonderful woman after his time in the service, but was later confined to a wheelchair during treatment at the Sam Rayburn VA Memorial Center in Bonham, Texas.

Both he and I gave our all for our country and I am so pleased to see the progress that the U.S. has made in race relations. It has been especially gratifying to see us elect a black president.

Yet decades before Barack Obama became a leader of all people in America, I and others in the Armed Forces helped to introduce white people to all that black people had to offer, a significant event in our country's racial history. My time in the service changed my life after I nearly lost it. It was an honor to be entrusted with the privilege of leading men into battle, to spearhead secret missions, to only be known to others as HB.

I received the Army of Occupation Medal (Japan), a World War II Victory Medal, a Good Conduct Medal, and an Asiatic Pacific Theatre Ribbon for my distinguished service to my country.

I'm overjoyed to be able to pen this memoir, thanks to the wonderful care that Dr. May and others gave to me, halfway around the world from my home.

Truly, his tears conquered my pains.

Whose pains are you helping to conquer?